T0366465

GIFTED GREEK

ADST-DACOR Diplomats and Diplomacy Series

Series Editor: MARGERY BOICHEL THOMPSON

SINCE 1776, EXTRAORDINARY men and women have represented the United States abroad under widely varying circumstances.
What they did and how and why they did it remain little known
to their compatriots. In 1995, the Association for Diplomatic Studies and Training (ADST) and DACOR, an organization of foreign
affairs professionals, created the Diplomats and Diplomacy book
series to increase public knowledge and appreciation of the profes-
sionalism of American diplomats and their involvement in world
history. Over thirty years and three assignments to Athens, Ambassador Monteagle "Monty" Stearns, one of America's most admired
diplomats, witnessed the transformation of Greece's first socialist prime minister from affable American economist to fiery anti-
American Greek politician. Stearns's character study of Andreas
Papandreou is the seventy-first volume in the series.

GIFTED GREEK

The Enigma of
Andreas Papandreou

Monteagle Stearns

An ADST-DACOR Diplomats and Diplomacy Book

Potomac Books

AN IMPRINT OF THE UNIVERSITY OF NEBRASKA PRESS

The opinions and characterizations in this book are those of
the author and do not necessarily reflect the opinions of the
United States government, the Association for Diplomatic
Studies and Training, or DACOR.

Library of Congress Cataloging-in-Publication Data
Names: Stearns, Monteagle, 1924–2016 author.
Title: Gifted Greek: the enigma of Andreas Papandreou /
Monteagle Stearns.
Description: Lincoln: Potomac Books, an imprint of the
University of Nebraska Press, 2021. | Series: ADST-DACOR
diplomats and diplomacy series. | Includes bibliographical
references.
Identifiers: LCCN 2020021090
ISBN 9781640123298 (hardback)
ISBN 9781640124233 (epub)
ISBN 9781640124240 (mobi)
ISBN 9781640124257 (pdf)
Subjects: LCSH: Papandreou, Andreas George. | Prime
ministers—Greece—Biography. | Greece—Politics
and government—1935–1967. | Greece—Politics and
government—1967–1974. | Greece—Politics and
government—1974–
Classification: LCC DF854.32.P36 S74 2021
DDC 949.507/6092 [B]—dc23
LC record available at https://lccn.loc.gov/2020021090

Set in Garamond Premier by Laura Buis.

Contents

List of Illustrations......vii

Foreword by Antonia R. Stearns......ix

Introduction......xiii

1. The Past Is Never the Past......1

2. Building a Future......21

3. Personal and Postwar Developments......39

4. Romance and Return......43

5. The Years of Our Greek Experience......56

6. Crises Everywhere......81

7. The Post-Junta Scene......89

8. Prime Time......97

Epilogue......131

Notes......137

Illustrations

Following page 42

1. Andreas Papandreou with the author and his wife, circa 1960

2. Three generations of Greek prime ministers, circa 1960

3. Andreas and Margaret Papandreou and their children in Canada, circa 1971

4. Andreas greeted by enthusiastic crowds after his exile and return to Athens, 1974

5. Andreas's star rises

6. Papandreou is received by Constantine Karamanlis

7. The author's first call on the newly elected prime minister causes a media frenzy

8. Old acquaintances manage a friendly handshake

9. Presentation of credentials to President Karamanlis

10. Melina Mercouri, with the author and his wife, 1983

11. Aged rivals' last premiership and presidency, 1994

Foreword

ANTONIA R. STEARNS

AMONG MANY TALENTS, my husband, Monty, was a gifted writer. He honed his reportorial skills in the Foreign Service but had been practicing them since fifth grade, when he composed, mimeographed, and peddled to the neighbors his satirical paper, *The Screwy News*. A voracious reader of all genres, he majored in English literature, and while serving in the Marine Corps, spent his off-duty hours with a rented typewriter, trying his hand at the Great American Novel.

Monty's other passion was the cinema. Fresh out of college he took a job reviewing documentary films and went on to work as a motion picture officer for the U.S. Information Agency, then considered something of an upstart newcomer by the State Department's old-school diplomats. His first posting was to Turkey, where he roamed the hinterlands in a jeep and showed films on the virtues of American democracy to puzzled villagers and the occasional sheep. In time his perceptive reports on Anatolian conditions and attitudes caught the eye of our ambassador in Ankara. Summoning Monty to his office, he asked imperiously why he was working for USIA. "My dear boy, you're a born political analyst and my advice to you is to give up this silly propaganda business, take the Foreign Service exams, and come in through the front door."

Throughout his diplomatic career and later in academia, Monty published numerous articles and two books on American foreign policy, all in the voice of the omniscient narrator. *Gifted Greek*: *The*

Enigma of Andreas Papandreou, however, is a much more personal book: a memoir and character study of Greece's first socialist prime minister, whose transformation from affable American economist to fiery, anti-American Greek politician Monty witnessed at close hand during three assignments to Athens, the last as U.S. ambassador.

The book is also a reflection on the Cold War era, its impact on Greek and American relations, and especially its impact on Andreas Papandreou, whom we met in Athens in 1959. Born and raised in Greece but a naturalized American citizen since 1945, Andreas was then chairman of the economics department at the University of California, Berkeley. At the invitation of the Greek government, he was spending a sabbatical year in Athens, studying Greece's backward economy and preparing a report on how to improve it.

As fellow Americans, coincidentally living on the same street, we soon became good friends with "Andy and Maggie"—as Andreas and his midwestern wife, Margaret, still called themselves—swapping cups of sugar along with like-minded impressions of Greece. It was easy to praise its scenic beauties and agreeable way of life; less so to find a good word for its inefficient bureaucracy and Byzantine political system. Andreas, who had to deal with both, regaled us with tales of lost files, cooked figures, and incompetent officials—all of which left him in a quandary over whether to finish his report and go back to California or extend his stay and push for his economic reforms to be enacted.

He was increasingly pressured by his father, a prominent Greek politician who had long wanted his son to return to Greece and become his political heir. Andreas was torn. To keep his options open, he set up and headed an economic research institute in Athens, all the while moving restlessly between his two homelands. We were his sounding board, and over many animated evenings the four of us talked late into the night about Andreas's future. Monty's efforts to dissuade him from plunging into Greece's political maelstrom proved futile, but their friendship remained solid.

In our subsequent tours in Athens, however, that friendship would be tested and frayed after Andreas's fateful decision to give up his

American citizenship and run for office in Greece, first as his father's ally and soon thereafter as his bitter rival. The psychological and political dramas that ensued, as he wrestled with his half-Greek, half-American instincts and identity, always fascinated Monty and led to this account of their curiously entwined personal and professional lives.

My involvement in bringing *Gifted Greek* to publication began when Monty could no longer see to type, becoming eventually too ill to incorporate his dictated revisions into the manuscript. Like any long-married couple, especially when both are writers, we argued about placement, wording, tone, and even the street numbers of the houses we'd lived in.

Still, we made a pretty good team, and shortly before his death Monty took my hand in his and said, "Only you know what I wanted to say and how to say it in my voice. Could you . . . would you?" There was no need to finish the sentence. I promised that I would, although six months passed before I could bring myself to look at the manuscript, much less the revisions, some of them complete, others trailing off in mid-dictation.

I read and reread them all, went to bed fretting over a redundancy here, a narrative gap there, until suddenly, one winter morning, I woke up with a complete segue in my head and raced in a tattered robe to my laptop. The muse—or was it Monty?—had landed on my shoulder, jogging my memory that a certain segue was already in the text and needed only to be moved elsewhere. From then on, the responsibility of keeping Monty's voice intact became more a matter of rearranging than rewriting, although I couldn't resist tightening the dialogue when it sounded more like a cablegram than a conversation.

And so the book now stands—I hope faithful to Monty's intentions, however much he needed a collaborator at the end. That he chose me seemed logical, and natural. After all, I married into the Foreign Service when its couples were known, cheerfully enough at the time, as two for the price of one. As a relic of that vanished era, I took on the assignment out of wifely duty but finished as a most satisfied partner, reliving shared experiences and Monty's keen observations of them in every chapter. In consequence, *Gifted Greek* has also proved a gift in perpetuity from Monty, to whom I write these words in loving memory of our long, adventurous, and happy years together.

Introduction

"WE ANGLO-SAXONS ARE bound to Greece by ties of landscape and history." So spoke the English poet Stephen Spender in his introductory remarks to a literary society in Athens, where I was a newly arrived political officer at the United States Embassy. It was a charming speech and somewhat quaint, as Athens still was in 1958. Over twenty years later, when I was on my third diplomatic posting to Athens, Spender's serene recollection of Greece would be hard to recognize in its concrete-filled landscape and frayed historical bonds.

Yet through all the changes the bonds remain. The founding fathers of the American Republic, no less than their British regents, were steeped in the history of ancient Greece. University and factory towns bearing the names of Athens, Sparta, Ithaca, and Syracuse are lingering traces of a more profound imprint made by colonial schoolmasters who placed the classical canon on a shelf next to the four Gospels. As for landscape, the rugged coastline of Greece, the silhouettes of myriad islands that seem from a distance bare and forbidding, still reveal upon arrival a picturesque scene of harbors and villages pulsing with human activity. Those stark outlines of mountain against sky, of cypress against sea, and sun over blinding white sugar cube houses are forever embedded in the foreigner's eye and emotions.

But Spender omitted a third feature of Greece as striking as its history or landscape: the Greeks themselves. Ebullient and garrulous, they are a hardy people whose bravery, astuteness, and resilience have enabled them—over the centuries and against great odds—to preserve their language, religion, and strong sense of national identity. Thanks to invading forebears from all directions there is much variety in that identity, but there are also distinctive traits that reach back to antiquity. Their legendary hospitality to strangers, curiosity about the world, and love of public life come to mind, but so do obstinacy, exaggerated pride, and impetuous behavior: bear in mind that Oedipus killed his father in a dispute over the right of way at a crossroad. It has to be said that the Greek temperament no more resembles the Anglo-Saxon one than Zorba resembles Sherlock Holmes.

Family loyalty, with all the comforts and constraints that it confers on the individual, is the cultural glue of Greekness, and while "family values" have become a popular political slogan in the United States today, they have been a way of life and the nucleus of social and political organization in Greece for centuries. Much as we Americans admire these core values at the personal level, on the larger stage of Greek-American relations the differences between our two cultures can often lead to exasperation and mutual incomprehension of each other's behavior.

Few Greeks in recent memory have aroused more exasperation in our foreign policy establishment than Andreas Papandreou. He first raised hackles leading a left wing (but noncommunist) movement in the 1960s and continued to do so in the 1980s and 1990s as an outspokenly socialist prime minister. Within the NATO community, Papandreou stood out as the sharpest critic of the United States and a persistent apologist for the Soviet Union's transgressions. He tilted openly toward the Palestinian Liberation Organization's intifadas and spoke admiringly of Saddam Hussein's economic and social policies in Iraq. To both Democratic and Republican administrations it was doubly galling that this Greek provocateur had been a naturalized American citizen and twenty-year resident of the United States.

His rival, and staunch defender of Greece's membership in NATO, was the conservative leader Constantine Karamanlis, a four-time prime minister and later president of the Hellenic Republic until Papandreou abruptly ousted him during his first premiership. These two men set the tone of Greek politics for almost thirty years, until the death of Papandreou in 1996 and Karamanlis two years later. Ironically, it was Karamanlis who initially brought Papandreou back to Athens from the United States.

After a decade of massive aid to Greece, the Eisenhower administration was concerned by the country's slow economic growth in comparison to Western Europe's, and Karamanlis was under pressure to take action. In 1959 he invited Andreas, then the chairman of the economics department at the University of California, Berkeley, to spend a sabbatical year in Greece studying its natural resources and how to market them more effectively.

The driving force behind the invitation, however, was Andreas's father, George Papandreou, a former prime minister himself, leader of the Liberal Party and perpetually frustrated opponent of Karamanlis. He was equally frustrated by his son's refusals, despite many entreaties, to give up his academic career, return to Greece, and go into politics. While Andreas supported the Liberal Party's progressive platform, he had shown little enthusiasm for participating in Greek politics, much less under his father's scrutiny.

A sabbatical year, however, was a different matter, an opportunity for his American wife and children to see his native land and for Andreas to prove his success as an economist to his father, who made no secret of his disdain for the profession. And so Andreas accepted the offer, all the while determined to avoid Greece's Byzantine politics, finish his report, and go home. Or so he said. Despite (or perhaps because of) his exposure to the inefficiency, obfuscation, and corruption that Greek governments are often prone to, Andreas was pondering a second return, this time to establish an independent economic research institute, which he envisaged as an instigator of real reform. How this decision led to joining and then breaking with his father is an Oedipal tale that weaves through this personal recollection of events.

I was drawn to write about Andreas because of his intriguingly dual nature. It was not just that he was a different character at different times but that the two characters were so contradictory. Both were shaped by raw ambition but also by inner conflicts between his Greek mentality and his American one. When we first met, Andreas was an affably progressive American economist, dispassionate observer of events, and faithful husband from Berkeley, California; within ten years he would become a strident Greek politician, fiery demagogue, and restless, chain-smoking adulterer from Athens, Greece. Yet he was never entirely one or the other, nor was his adult life in the United States ever disentangled from a stressful childhood in Greece.

For most Americans, the shelf life of foreign political leaders is short. They catch the public eye briefly, during periods of crisis, then disappear just as quickly. Conversely, Greeks obsess over political leaders, both foreign and domestic, and argue their virtues and vices long after they are gone. Yet in Greece, too, where the Papandreou name was as well-known as Roosevelt's in twentieth-century American politics, Andreas's death came almost as an anticlimax. In his last years he was a shrunken remnant of his former self and, after his third marriage to a much younger former airline attendant, something of an embarrassment to his followers. The obituaries noted his intellectual gifts and charismatic appeal to a new generation of Greek voters; recalled his rebellious youth; and tallied up the score on his transformative agenda, which, in hindsight, seemed less transformative than originally perceived.

Greece's highly partisan newspapers reported that either "a hundred thousand" or "over a million" mourners followed his casket to the cemetery, and for days after he was lauded or lambasted on their front pages. Still, even the sincerest tributes conveyed a sense of paradox: an implication that, for whatever reason, he had squandered more opportunities than he had grasped. Many of his early supporters were equally tentative in their judgments. If Papandreou had really intended to turn Greece into an independent, egalitarian, socialist state, then why, they asked, had he not stayed the course instead of tacking in so many opposite directions? This scaled-down evaluation so soon after his death is the enigmatic legacy of Andreas Papandreou, between the promise he brought to Greece and the pallor of his reputation today.

Between 1959 and 1963 I knew Andreas at close hand, then intermittently and more remotely until we met up again in Athens in 1974. The intervening years had been traumatic for Greece and for Andreas, who by 1964, had given up his American citizenship to run for his father's seat in Parliament. The dissensions, both political and psychological, that soon arose between them would contribute to the downfall of Greek democracy. In April 1967, a cabal of army colonels seized power—in Andreas's lasting opinion, with the connivance of the United States. He was arrested and jailed, released after eight months, and sent into exile—first to Sweden and then to Canada, where he was offered a position at York University. During his imprisonment, frantic appeals from his wife and friends to European capitals and to Washington, where Andreas had old ties to high officials in the Johnson administration, proved more helpful in procuring his freedom than any voices in Greece. True, the Junta cracked down on all dissenters, but Andreas had hoped for mass public uprisings against it and felt betrayed when none occurred. Perhaps embarrassed by the fact, he would later take pains to avoid crediting Washington's efforts on his behalf.

Andreas spent the next six years organizing a resistance movement against "the Colonels," as the Junta came to be called. At the same time he became a virulent critic of the Vietnam War, of the Nixon administration, in fact of everything the United States government stood for. From his base at York University, he traveled extensively, gathering fellow Greek exiles to the cause and drawing occasional media attention, while the Junta settled in for the duration. He grew sideburns, wore hippie attire, and spelled America with a *k*. His anti-Junta, antiestablishment crusade mirrored the social upheavals and protest movements of the time. After the Junta's fall, it would give him a base of support among disaffected Greeks, from students to blue collar workers and many who were simply sick of Greece's old guard, whether military or civilian. Between the 1974 and 1977 elections and again in 1981, Papandreou's new party, PASOK, doubled and redoubled its percentage of votes and parliamentary seats.

By 1981, when I returned to Athens for a third assignment, this time as American ambassador, Andreas was on the verge of becoming prime minister, running noisily on a platform ("Greece for the Greeks!") that pledged to free its subjects from American intervention in its affairs and assorted other historical perfidies. Fortunately, our long association took the brunt off what might otherwise have been an unpleasantly contentious relationship. And for all our professional controversies we were, in a way, still personal friends, with a similar sense of humor and lifestyle preferences: late nights over early mornings; taverna fare over nouvelle cuisine; '60s mellow jazz over '80s heavy metal. This, of course, was the American Andreas, but I never knew for sure if the Greek one would publicly reverse our private agreements—usually when hard-left PASOK cabinet ministers and parliamentarians found him too conciliatory toward Americans.

Few people born and raised in Greece, as Andreas was, go through life unaware of their country's geographic vulnerability and historical reliance on foreign powers to protect their independence. America's turn came in 1947 with the Truman Doctrine, which proclaimed a special security relationship between Greece and the United States. At the time Greece was in the throes of a polarizing civil war over its future political system. Throughout the Nazi occupation, a hodgepodge of republican, royalist, and communist resistance groups, the first two aided by the British, had continued to fight against the Germans—then increasingly against each other. At war's end, an exhausted Britain passed the torch to the United States, which began a massive assistance program to keep Greece safely locked into the Western alliance.

This alliance was not based exclusively on realpolitik. Our affectionate sentiment for the cradle of democracy was real and longstanding. Just as many Greeks had been inspired by the American

Revolution in the 1770s, so were many Americans by the Greek War of Independence in the 1820s. Thinking practically about the fledgling democracy's needs, they brought the first printing presses and medical supplies, built schools, and sent teachers to staff them. By the end of the nineteenth century a small colony of American philhellenes had followed their muse to Greece, from frock-coated archaeologists at the American School of Classical Studies (opened in 1881) to scantily clad bohemians frolicking in sacred groves.

Between 1947 and Greece's entry into NATO in 1952, the American presence in Greece grew exponentially. Legions of military and financial advisors bustled through Greek government offices; annexes to our embassy proliferated to accommodate specialists and spies; an American air force base employed more personnel than Athens's commercial airport just across the road. The opportunities and higher wages offered by the Americans led thousands of Greeks to spend their entire working lives in service to the United States.

Over time, powerful protectors begin to grate on the nerves of the protected, however much they are needed. Great Britain, France, and Tsarist Russia had all preceded the United States as guarantors of Greece's national security, but with greater experience. By long tradition Americans were isolationists and had paid scant attention to the Machiavellian alliances of the European powers, from whose "ambition, rivalship, interest, humor, or caprice" George Washington counseled us to remain detached. Today, of course, we are members of many alliances, but we have never lost the belief in our exceptionalism or the instinct to follow a unilateral approach in foreign policy.

The Greeks also believe in their own exceptionalism, but the basis for it is very different from the Americans'. We are a large continental nation and Greece a small maritime one. Our country has been shaped by abundance; theirs by insufficiency. We have never been occupied; the Greeks lived almost four hundred years under Ottoman (Turkish) suzerainty, during which they relied on blood ties for sustenance and on subterfuge against the practices of a corrupt and predatory sultanate. Law was arbitrary, capricious, and to be evaded whenever possible. Safety lay in concealment, not openness; in the unity of the clan, not the bureaucracy of the empire. Long after their independence, the Greeks continued their bitter hostility toward the Turks, and it was only briefly, when both faced Stalin's threat to build a naval base in the Dardanelles, that fear of Turkey was not the dominant consideration in Greek foreign policy.

Relations between Ankara and Athens reached a nadir in 1955, when disputes over the future status of Cyprus led to anti-Greek riots in Istanbul and Izmir and the virtual elimination of the remaining Greek community in Turkey. That the two countries were members of NATO further complicated matters. Washington, reluctant to be drawn into the fray and trying to avoid antagonizing either side, usually succeeded in antagonizing both. The pragmatic Turks would make the necessary protests and then go back to business as usual, whereas the Greeks suffered emotional meltdowns over our well-intentioned neutrality. Were we not their protector and they our faithful ally? From 1950s riots to later crises over air and sea incursions, competing claims over uninhabited Aegean rocks, and the Cyprus stalemate, the Greeks remained convinced that the United States had failed to give them the support they deserved in their grievances against the Turks. We were like family who had let them down.

At this point in my story I should add that much has changed in the twenty-first century. These days the Greeks vent their disappointed expectations on the European Union, formerly the European Economic Community (EEC), which their country joined in January 1981, while Karamanlis was still prime minister. Always a believer that the future of Greek democracy lay in closer ties to Western Europe, Karamanlis had pushed hard for admission since 1974, and his success proved a boon for Andreas. Despite his pledge to take Greece out of the EU, Papandreou drew recklessly on its generous financial loans to pay for his lavish (although sorely needed) social welfare programs. But he neglected to offset the deficits by raising taxes—much less by reforming the corrupt taxation system as a whole.

Nor did his successors. Despite Andreas's electoral defeat in

1989, after his illegal efforts to replenish the treasury's empty coffers had been exposed, both conservative and socialist governments were loath to cut the higher wages, pensions, and expanded welfare programs that Greek voters were now happily accustomed to. For the next twenty years budget deficits continued to mount, and the Greeks continued to believe they were richer than they actually were, until the 2008 global financial crisis revealed their county's astronomical budget deficits. The crisis led the EU to impose harsh austerity measures from which Greece has yet to recover. It also led to the downfall of PASOK and its leader, Andreas's eldest son, George Papandreou Jr., who paid the price of his father's failure to take economics as seriously as politics. Once again, Greece has become the "Poor Man of Europe."

That Greece has managed to survive its recurring economic difficulties is partly due to emigration, particularly between 1890 and 1914, when a sixth of the Greek population, mostly rural (and with encouragement from conservative governments in Athens) emigrated abroad, the majority to the United States, and joined the great influx of Eastern Europeans, Italians, and Jews fleeing poverty and persecution in their homelands. Some Greek arrivals failed to thrive in America's competitive culture; others surmounted the challenges but dreamed of returning to Greece in their old age. When I first traveled in the Greek countryside, I was invariably introduced to the local Amerikanos, an elderly villager living off his social security checks, speaking outdated English, and keen to ask if I knew his cousin in . . . (name any American city). But the great majority remained for life, prospered, and became exemplars of the immigrant success story: entering the professional ranks, acquiring property, and sending their offspring to college with remarkable speed.

In contrast, Andreas Papandreou's American experience was not that of an immigrant but of an exile, and a very well-educated one at that. He had excelled at Athens College, an elite preparatory school for Athens's upper bourgeoisie, and had completed two years of law school before leaving for the United States. He had also, however, grown up during the Great Depression and the Metaxas dictatorship, a copycat fascist regime that ruled Greece from 1936 to 1941, and his adolescent politics were avowedly left wing. In 1939 he was arrested and brutally beaten for his subversive Trotskyite activities, and to avoid future persecution he left Greece in 1940. The timing was serendipitous. Shortly afterward Greece was invaded by the Italians, then overrun by the Germans. For almost two decades the Greeks would endure Nazi occupation, starvation, a civil war, hyperinflation, and a painful economic recovery before Andreas returned in 1959.

Yet to all intents and purposes those two decades seemed to have passed him by. When Andreas began graduate studies at Harvard, he quickly shed (or concealed) his adolescent Trotskyism and devoted himself to study. After receiving his PhD in economics he enlisted in the U.S. Navy and applied for American citizenship, which was granted shortly before his discharge in 1945.

While Andreas was in American uniform, George Papandreou had escaped Athens and was living in Cairo as a member of the Greek government-in-exile. Arguments over which of its members would lead Greece after the country's liberation were eventually settled by the British, who appointed Papandreou prime minister in 1944. Under their protection, he would return in triumph to Athens and govern briefly between the Germans' retreat and the full-scale outbreak of civil war.

Again, Greece's troubles appear to have made little impact on Andreas, perhaps because he had troubles of his own. In early 1941, too soon and for misguided reasons, he had married a young Greek American woman, Christina Rassia, the daughter of an overbearing father and a socially ambitious mother. Their unhappy union dragged on until their divorce in 1951—after which Andreas immediately married Margaret Chant, his paramour since 1948.

In 1953, a much happier and more relaxed Andreas took Margaret for a holiday in Greece, to introduce her to his father and the usual sites. A few days into the visit Andreas suddenly and inexplicably developed a severe pain in his jaw, so paralyzing and so affecting his emotional state that the couple had to break off their holiday and go home. This was the first of future ailments that armchair analysts might attribute to suppressed memories, generally of his difficult relations with his father, and specifically of the broken jaw he had suffered at the hands of the Metaxas police during their interrogation of him in 1939.

Suppressed memories may also have lain behind Andreas's seeming indifference to the critical economic and political issues facing the allies during World War II and its aftermath. His 1943 doctoral thesis, "The Location and Scope of the Entrepreneurial Function," was an analysis of control and decision-making in major American corporations. In the 1950s he wrote frequently about macroeconomic theory, relying heavily on mathematical formulations that conveyed no obvious political leanings. And so disinterested did he appear about events in Greece that a colleague at the University of California, who had his Greek newspapers delivered to Andreas while he was on vacation, returned a month later to find them unopened. This, furthermore, was the period leading up to the pivotal 1958 Greek elections in which his father's Liberal Party lost its usual second-place finish to the communists, threatening the conservative regimes that had held sway over Greece for decades. At about the same time Andreas was writing *A Test of a Stochastic Theory of Choice*, a less-than-page-turning study of the randomness factor in economic decision-making.

In my first conversations with Andreas he was focused on his research project on the Greek economy and how little attention Greek politicians paid to it. As we became better acquainted, I realized that among those politicians Andreas did not exclude George Papandreou, to judge from his amused—or bemused—reactions to his father's low opinion of professional economists. Since I was also the son of a distant father who took no interest in my chosen profession, I could sympathize with Andreas's ambivalent feelings.

By virtue of my embassy assignment, which was to cover the goings on in the Liberal Party, I had met the father before the son. I had my own bemused reaction to how readily the elder Papandreou welcomed me, an obscure American diplomat with rudimentary Greek trying to make sense of Greece's complex and constantly shifting political coalitions. But such was our embassy's influence at the time, and so anxious was Papandreou to be taken seriously by it as a potential successor to Karamanlis, that his door was always open. Furthermore, the fact that I would shortly befriend Andreas made me a useful figure, in the father's view, as a conduit to the son and as a helpful interlocutor in his campaign to keep Andreas in Greece.

And so my wife, Toni, and I often joined Margaret and Andreas for dinner at George Papandreou's villa in Kastri, a bucolic suburb of Athens. The conversation dwelt almost exclusively on the Liberal Party's prospects of defeating the conservative party, the contrarily named National Radical Union (ERE in Greek). I scooped my colleagues taking mental notes as Papandreou spoke openly about ERE dissenters and his plans to form a coalition with them under the banner of a new party, which within a year became the Center Union. Papandreou would hold forth lengthily in Greek, then pause for Andreas to summarize his train of thought in English, lest I miss the import of his message.

Throughout his sabbatical year we noticed Andreas's diffidence toward his father. "*Nai, patera*" (Yes, father) he would say politely, even when he disagreed, and "*Sygnomi, patera*" (Excuse me, father) before venturing a cautious opinion of his own. We also noticed an absence of domestic chitchat, an unusual omission at Greek family gatherings, but then Andreas had reason to be wary. One Sunday he showed up unexpectedly at our house, flushed and in need of a drink after an unpleasant scene with his father, who had dropped by without warning and found Andreas outside, washing his car. Infuriated, he yanked the hose from Andreas's hands and thundered, "You might do this in America, but in Greece a prime minister's son does *not* wash his car!" It was the Greek father admonishing the American son.

Conversely, in his exile years in Canada, Andreas began to mirror his father's imperiousness. In a conversation with Margaret, two years after Andreas's death, she told me how angry he became if his children spoke to him in what he considered an impertinent

Introduction

manner. "You must teach them *respect*," he lectured her. Margaret replied testily that where she came from respect was not taught but earned. It was the American wife admonishing her Greek husband. Trivial incidents perhaps, but illustrative of ingrained behavior patterns that lead me to reflect on American culture and to what extent it can be implanted elsewhere.

I pose this in the broader context of an attempt to reassess the goals of American foreign policy in the twenty-first century. The belief that our form of government, our way of life, is the answer to the world's ills fails to take note of resurgent cultural and nationalist movements in Europe, fragile states in Africa and the Middle East, and spreading stateless terrorism—leaving us unsure if our response should be military engagement, proxy wars, retrenchment, or extended "soft diplomacy" campaigns to promote American values in countries very unlike our own. The debate goes on.

The story of Andreas Papandreou is perhaps only a short chapter in that debate, but he remains an intriguing study of success and failure in two careers and two countries. As a respected American economist he inflicted disastrous economic policies on Greece; as a Greek politician he campaigned for democratic reforms, only to embrace the patronage system he had once decried, maintaining his power through clientelism, financial chicanery, and the cult of personality. Today, for many young people, the populist uprisings in nineteenth-century Greece and 1960s America have faded into the past, along with Papandreou himself. In the end, he proved to be less a principled crusader than a cynical politician, more ambitious than idealistic. But who would call that more Greek than American?

GIFTED GREEK

I

The Past Is Never the Past

ANDREAS HAD JUST turned seventeen when he submitted his first (and perhaps only) poem to his school's literary publication, *The Athenian*.

My Inner Self
BY A. G. PAPANDREOU

Sometimes when I stop and think a little, I think about myself
And indeed I tell you, I see something very different from what you see.

I do not present this boy to you as he really is. No, I don't have the courage to do so.

I [try] to show you a man of high mental powers, a philosopher, a great writer, a social reformer, and in some ways I am.

I have some good things to say about myself, but in general, when I am alone with myself I am merely a man. I eat, I drink, I take pleasure in seeing the sun rise.

And lastly I am full of human passions which I try to hide.

Ah! How I should like a world in which good men are met, in which the outside and the inside coincide, a world in which man would be free enough to show himself and good enough to be worth looking at.

What adolescent male hasn't agonized over his hidden self, not to mention his hormones? But in this poem Andreas seems to be using personal anxiety to conceal his political thoughts. A precocious teenager in the 1930s, Andreas (like so many of the era's disillusioned adults) was caught up in the events of that ominous decade and heavily influenced by Marxist ideology. A star student, first in his class—albeit after a rocky start in elementary school—he grew up in the Athens suburb of Psychiko, in a house his mother, Sophia, purchased in the early 1920s.

The family had moved back to the Greek capital from Chios, where Andreas was born on February 5, 1919. At the time George Papandreou was governor of the Aegean Islands and a rising member of the Liberal Party, founded by the great republican leader Eleftherios Venizelos. He would hold a series of high positions in republican administrations, return to his law practice during royalist ones, and gain a name for himself as something of a Don Juan. George's affairs and frequent absences took their toll on Sophia and on Andreas, who was ten when his father abandoned them for good and took up with a glamorous (and soon pregnant) stage actress, the one-named Kyveli. They settled in Kastri, a still-countrified suburb north of Athens.

Sophia Mineiko Papandreou was the daughter of a Greek mother and a Lithuanian Polish father, Sygmund Mineiko. As an officer in the Polish army's Corps of Engineers, he had been decorated for bravery and (according to family lore) been ennobled with the title of count. In the late nineteenth century Mineiko was engaged by the Ottomans to oversee repairs to their fortifications in what is today Albania and in the region around Ioannina, not yet united with the Greek state. There, he met his future wife, Prosperina Manaris, and by the time they married his loyalty had shifted from the crumbling Ottoman Empire to the Greeks. The couple moved to Athens, where Mineiko offered his services to the Greek army. In the Balkan Wars of 1912 and 1913 the Greeks were able to capture Ioannina, thanks to foreknowledge of its defenses that Mineiko himself had drawn up for the Turks. For this he was again decorated, this time by King Constantine of Greece. Two medals and a title to his name notwithstanding, Mineiko was anything but a royalist, and his belief that Greece would fare better as a republic was strengthened during the on-again, off-again regimes of kings Constantine I, Alexander, and George II.

But regime change was the norm and had been since the country achieved independence from the Ottomans. The history of modern Greek democracy has been as tarnished as its classical origins were lustrous. After the War of Independence the victors immediately fell to squabbling, sometimes at pistol point, over how and by whom the piecemeal nation should be governed. The issue was settled by the three great powers of the time (Great Britain, France, and Russia), who believed that national unity would be achieved by establishing a constitutional monarchy. Unfortunately, they failed to consult with the Greeks themselves, many of whom wanted a republic. With the form of government already a divisive issue, Greece's first hundred years as a nation-state were marked by violence, abdication, assassination, and political buccaneering.

The first monarch chosen by the great powers was a Bavarian import, Prince Otto, soon to be crowned Othon, king of the Greeks. Young Otto arrived with much fanfare on a British warship in 1832 and departed ignominiously on another one thirty years later. A second import, this time from Denmark, George I, enjoyed a lengthier reign, but his heirs came and went with alarming frequency until the monarchy was finally abolished in 1974. The underlying friction between its supporters and opponents dominated political debate.

But with or without a monarchy, the Greeks' ingrained habit of putting family interests above national ones—and of supporting local favorites to attain them—led to the growth of political dynasties (both royalist and republican) whose entrenched power relied on favors to their constituents and the backing of wealthy patrons in Europe as well as Greece. Drawn primarily from the upper bourgeoisie, they ignored the needs of the laboring class, which would eventually and spasmodically organize itself in trade unions and political parties heavily influenced by Marxist thinking.

Although not part of the political establishment, Sygmund Mineiko prospered in both government and private service. An accomplished architectural engineer, he was called upon to design many public buildings, as well as the stadium for the first modern Olympic Games (held in 1896). By this time he was a proud Greek citizen and father of numerous children. (Seven, by some accounts; six in others.)

Born in 1883, Sygmund's second child, Sophia Mineiko, was raised in comfort. Two of her sisters married into the Polish gentry, but like her father, Sophia was anti-monarchist and found no suitors in Athens's conservative social circles. She met George Papandreou when he was a law student at the University of Athens and was promptly smitten. Her parents were not overjoyed with the match, but by then Sophia was in her late twenties, approaching spinsterhood, and they were probably relieved that a man five years younger than their daughter had asked for her hand.

For George Papandreou the marriage was a step up, socially and financially. He was born in 1888 in Kalendzi, a village in Achaea province, where his father was the head priest (*presvyteros*) of a mountainous district overlooking the port city of Patras. Handsome, intelligent, and ambitious, with a stentorian voice and a gift for oratory, George Papandreou rose beyond his provincial roots to study law in Athens and philosophy in Germany, where he developed an abiding faith in the principles of democratic socialism.

His faith in marriage vows, however, was considerably less abiding and may have contributed to Sophia's postpartum depression after she gave birth to her only child at the age of thirty-six. She separated from Papandreou, retreated into the role of devoted mother, and when Kyveli became pregnant, filed for divorce in 1929. Whatever bitterness she may have felt, she never spoke ill of her errant husband over the many decades she would come to live with Andreas and his family—although Andreas's first wife, Christina Rassia, with whom Sophia also lived for brief periods, suspected that her mother-in-law's Orthodox piety was a kind of therapy to repress vengeful thoughts. George Papandreou was less circumspect about their marriage and in later years, when Andreas had become his political rival, belittled Sophia as the cause of Andreas's character flaws. "He is secretive and impulsive," he once told Margaret Papandreou, adding, "Those are Mineiko traits."[1]

Whatever side they came from, Andreas's early flaws were inattentiveness and disruptive behavior in elementary school. After he repeatedly brought home abysmal report cards, Sophia withdrew him from school and had him tutored at home. Still unhappy with his performance, George Papandreou stepped in and enrolled Andreas in Athens College, one of the best (and best known) private schools in Greece. Established in 1925, Athens College was an extended version of an American preparatory school, with an earlier entrance year (third grade) and an optional thirteenth year to polish the final product.

Athens College offered its boy students an educational standard considerably higher and more progressive than Greece's state schools, where students learned by rote and few went on to university. In addition, textbooks were often rewritten by the Ministry of Education according to the whims of which government was in power; in Andreas's youth one could hardly keep track of the changes.

By the early 1920s Eleftherios Venizelos had been defeated at the polls; his disastrous military campaign to extend Greece's borders into mainland Turkey had left the Greek army routed by Kemal Ataturk and Izmir's Greek population put to flight or to death. Athens was in turmoil following the unexpected death of King Alexander (from a monkey bite); and a coup soon followed. A gang of antimonarchist army officers executed a group of rivals, both civilian and military, accused of having supported the king during the failed Asia Minor campaign. In 1924 a plebiscite abolished the monarchy and for the next twelve years Greece was ruled as a republic, albeit an unstable one, with the military playing a large role in civilian affairs.

It was in this climate that several wealthy and influential Greek families built Athens College, in conjunction with American educators, many of them drawn from older American-founded schools in Asia Minor. The college operated under an American president, a mix of Greek and anglophone faculty, and classes that stressed independent thinking and civic responsibility based on the American pedagogic model.

It was not, however, an egalitarian model. Like England's public (i.e., private) schools and American preparatory schools (their names often compressed into "St. Grottlesex"), the purpose of the college was to educate the elite in their duty to lead the non-elite. Since its founding, the college has certainly produced its share of leaders, Papandreou among them, but it would also become a perennial target of criticism from the Greek left as a cradle of privilege and exclusion. (In the 1960s Andreas did not hesitate to enroll his sons there; as prime minister in the 1980s, however, he shunned any reference to it and was conspicuously silent when his party denounced American private schools, of which there were now several, as incompatible with true socialism.)

Greek students spent six years in *demotikon* (grades one through six) and another six in *gymnasion* (grades seven through twelve). After completing, however indifferently, four years in elementary school, Andreas entered Athens College in the fifth *demotikon*, still badly behaved and older than his classmates, having lost a year when he was sent to a Swiss sanatorium for a suspected case of tuberculosis. He would later recount that he loved the time he spent in an Alpine sanatorium and benefited by learning French in the process. But despite that advantage, and two years of private tutoring, his academic performance was so poor that the college threatened to expel him. Upon hearing the news, George Papandreou took umbrage at the disgrace his son was bringing to the family name. According to Christina Rassia's memoir, the upright father stormed from his love nest in Kastri to his son's bedroom in Psychiko and delivered a lecture so filled with anger and disappointment that the eleven-year-old boy sobbed uncontrollably for the rest of the night.[2]

The impact of his father's admonition was immediate. All summer Andreas worked doggedly to prepare for the next academic year, with the result that he moved from ranking last in his fifth-year class to finishing first in his sixth. He would remain at the top thereafter, from Athens College to the University of Athens and Harvard. The college's high standards undoubtedly suited—and challenged—his intellectual gifts, and in that respect, he found a measure of rapport with his father, who oversaw his academic progress at periodic Sunday lunches together in Kastri. There, the elder Papandreou introduced him to his library, which was largely stocked with books on political history and theory. By his third year of *gymnasion* Andreas, not yet fifteen, was well versed in the lessons of history, from the fall of Rome to the French Revolution and nineteenth-century European socialism. One day he dipped into Marx and Engel's *Communist Manifesto* and became so absorbed that he borrowed it to read at home.

It was an intellectual epiphany. To Andreas, Marxism brilliantly foretold the Great Depression and the internal contradictions of capitalism that would bring about its collapse. Andreas's mathematical bent and attraction to "scientific" economic models (that would infuse much of his academic writing) could only have added to his sense of discovery. He was too young, of course, to see the irony that in its claim to be "scientific," Marxism acquired all the dogma of religious belief. In his classic work, *Russia in Flux*, Sir John Maynard (1864–1943) analyzed the contradictions of Marxist thought:

> Marx called his own Socialism *scientific*, and the earlier Socialism *utopian* because he [Marx] made a new departure in this respect. He plotted the curve of history, as mathematicians say, and his prophecy was its continuation. It is this plotting of the curve of history that is the essence of the Marxian method. And the method is more important than any of the results so far attained by it. For without the method, prophecy degenerates into dogma and, if right, is only right by accident or inspiration. With the method, if it be sound, there is a vista of further results, ascertaining, perhaps controlling, the evolution of human society.[3]

In his youth George Papandreou was also drawn to Marxism but rejected it thoroughly in the Venizelos era when he saw firsthand the ruthless practices Greek communists employed once gaining access to the state machinery. Lest his son be led astray, he hired a tutor to instruct Andreas on the shortcomings of Marxist ideology. The results were mixed. According to an account in the Greek journal *Pondiki*, Andreas, on his own initiative, also met regularly with a Marxist-leaning member of his father's circle named Skouriotis, who would point out the fallacies posited as truths by the other tutor.[4] In the *Pondiki* interview Andreas goes on to say: "In this way I learned about such concepts as 'value' and 'surplus value.' I was very young. What did I know about economics? But my sessions with Skouriotis gave me counter arguments to use with my father."[5] In 1934, after completing his third year of *gymnasion*, Andreas's Marxist sympathies led to an incident that again almost got him expelled from Athens College, this time for his political views.

The trouble began when a young instructor, George Phylactopoulos, met with Andreas and a fellow classmate to suggest some books for summer reading. Phylactopoulos would later become a legendary teacher at Athens College, dean of studies, and a beloved mentor to his students—but that day his future was seriously jeopardized. In an oral history published in 1992, Phylactopoulos recalled Andreas's near eviction, and his own:

> I was his instructor when he started a student magazine named *Xeki-nima* [The Setting Forth]. Andreas had perhaps the highest academic average [in the class]. He was very smart. And there was another boy with him, Paris Constantinides, who became a famous doctor in Canada, first, then the United States.... I gave them books like More's *Utopia* and Malthus. When ... they came to offer me the first edition of their magazine ... I told them how glad I would be to read it and so forth ... but I admit I did not read it fully.... I put it aside, but I wrote a note ... to congratulate them.[6]

Perhaps because of the approaching summer holidays the first issue of *Xekinima* managed to slip by scrutiny. But the second issue, scheduled for publication in October 1934, provoked a storm. Papandreou and Constantinides had not submitted their journal for faculty review, as college regulations required, and there were gasps of astonishment when Andreas's article, "The Economic Relationship of the Classes," appeared on the front page. The late MIT scientist and Athens College alumnus Dr. Michael Macrakis, who traced Andreas's intellectual development between 1933 and 1943, cites the article as a textbook example of teenage Marxism:

> The present economic system, the product of a bourgeois society, is today experiencing its greatest crisis. The free market economy leaves the individual unrestrained by any control, enabling the [entrepreneur] to rise above others, [his progress] based on individual interest and shameless deception. Over-production [gluts] the system and creates the present crisis. But, as Marx states, "The bourgeoisie produce not only their arms but the gravediggers who will use them, today's proletariat."

Andreas ended his article with an exhortation that must have curdled the blood of the good burghers on the board of directors. "We are obliged to join with Marx in saying, 'Workers of the world, unite!'"[7]

What made the publication particularly awkward for George Phylactopoulos was an editorial note warmly thanking him "for his encouragement of our work." Not only were students of Athens College propagating Marxism, the faculty was leading them down the revolutionary path!

The *Xekinima* issue, however minuscule its readership, seriously offended the college's benefactors. More seriously, and unbelievably to anyone unfamiliar with the petty concerns of the Greek political establishment, the article also drew the ire of the royalist-leaning government that had been elected the same year. The American president of Athens College, Homer W. Davis, felt obliged to confiscate the second issue to avoid spreading the controversy beyond the campus. He was too late. An outraged member of the college's board of directors had already leaked copies to the conservative press. Two newspapers, *Estia* and *Vradyni*, demanded immediate expulsion of the two student editors and of the instructor who had encouraged such incendiary writing. The Ministry of Education hastily announced that it would investigate the deplorable incident.

Davis had been president of Athens College since its inception, but this was his first clash with both his board and the Greek government. While his mission was to encourage independent thinking in his students, what most of the trustees (and parents) really had in mind was not so much independent thinking as a first-rate education that would ensure the superior position of their own class. As Davis later wrote, "They [the trustees] envisaged a school that would not be foreign legally or in spirit—a Greek school, Orthodox in religion, with American sponsorship and leadership."[8]

The proposition that Athens College could be both American in thought and Greek in spirit put Davis in a quandary. He believed that the institutional integrity of the college required him to resist political censorship of student beliefs by the government. "Our attitude," he wrote windily, "was that the very objectionable articles were the expression of intellectually precocious but immature youngsters whose previous records had been exemplary and who had been ill-advised or neglected by their parents and we sought the most effective ways of reasoning with them rather than making martyrs of them, thus risking hardening them in what we hoped was a passing phase of a kind that youth is prone to."[9]

Davis won his case with the trustees, but since it was based on "parental neglect" he felt obliged to call on George Papandreou and ask him, as a father, a former minister of education, and staunch anti-communist, to support the college and exonerate it from the government's charge of fostering Marxist ideology in the classroom.

To his dismay, George Papandreou was nonchalant to the point of indifference about the attacks on his son and on the college. He refused to issue any statement of support, leaving Davis to sigh, "It was no doubt naive of us to expect that a politician would make such a statement since it would imply that he, as a parent, accepted the responsibility which, as a matter of fact, we felt was largely his. We were certainly justified, however, in counting on a serious discussion of the subject." Instead, George Papandreou "brush[ed] aside the whole affair as being an attack on *him* by *his* political enemies and an attack on the College only because it had been founded and supported by prominent Venizelists. Had we not noticed, he asked, that another school, attended by a third editor of the magazine had *not* been attacked?" (Author's italics)

Davis then asked Papandreou how his son had developed his Marxist ideology. "The gist of his reply," Davis recorded, "was that at a time of such oppressive black reaction imposed on the country by the present government, young people naturally had to have something to look forward to and this led them to use exaggerated and immature language."[10] (In contrast to George Papandreou, Andreas's mother wrote an unsolicited letter to Davis to make clear that she did not hold the school responsible for her son's views.)

The *Xekinima* kerfuffle seems more significant for what it says of George Papandreou's vanity than of Andreas's upbringing. Fortunately for him, and for the college, the press soon turned to other scandals, of which there were no dearth in Greek politics, and public interest in the dangerous student perpetrators of Marxist philosophy faded away.

Once he became a political figure Andreas rarely referred to his Athens College days. When asked by a journalist in 1994 what his recollections of the college were, especially of his exposure to American teachers and the American educational system, he drew a contrast between the institution in the 1930s and the values of the United States sixty years later: "Americans in those days were entirely different. It was a period of great [economic] crisis in the United States. Young people got their doctorates and had nowhere to go. There was no work and so they came to Greece [to teach at the college] for a scrap of bread. To be given a job as a professor was something marvelous. They were all very young. Besides, the United States was not then an imperialist power."[11]

In 1935 the government held a plebiscite to determine whether King George II, living in comfortable exile at Brown's Hotel in London, should be restored to the throne. When the returns showed a majority vote in his favor, Andreas and a group of friends prepared to circulate a proclamation protesting the king's return.[12] According to Andreas, they were again thwarted by college authorities, who had already gotten wind of the proclamation and again threatened the boys with immediate expulsion. (One wonders if President Davis was losing tolerance for freedom of expression or if Andreas was simply exaggerating a protest that never got off the ground.) Threatened or not, Andreas and his friends made a tactical retreat: "The results of circulating the proclamation among a few students would not have been significant and we decided to lie low. We didn't distribute it."[13] In later years Papandreou's penchant for tactical retreats would frustrate his most ardent supporters almost as much as his proclamations infuriated his adversaries.

For reasons never made clear, Andreas left Athens College before completing his last year of *gymnasion* and enrolled in an experimental school (*peiramatiko scholeio*) that Athens University had recently established for gifted students. The fact that he was somewhat older than his classmates may have contributed to his decision, or that some of his friends were also leaving. In the event, Andreas spent the academic year 1936–37 at the *peiramatiko scholeio* and then entered the University of Athens in the fall.

As at Athens College, his academic record at the experimental school was outstanding. Professor John Stamatakos, who evaluated his performance at the end of the term, noted his "diligence and love of learning," his "retentive memory, excellent reasoning powers, and a desire to come to grips with the fundamental problems of life." His only weakness, Stamatakos observed, was a tendency to "demagogy and sophistry in discussion," characteristics that "might be attributed to his upbringing and inheritance." Nevertheless, he was personable, popular with his fellow students, and created no problems for his teachers. Like them, Stamatakos considered Papandreou one of a handful of the most serious and promising students he had encountered.[14]

Before leaving the *peiramatiko scholeio* Andreas completed a questionnaire about his professional aspirations. In descending order of preference, he wrote that he would like to become a politician, a sociologist, or (perhaps in jest) a sea captain. The first choice, he explained, reflected his desire to put his ideas into action; the second reflected his main intellectual interest, and if neither of these ambitions were realized, he would prefer travel and the sea to anything else. Rather surprisingly, Andreas listed teaching as his least favored profession. It would be "too tiring," he wrote, perhaps cognizant of the time and effort his own tutors and teachers had shown toward him. But in response to another question, he said that his greatest satisfaction would be to see the overthrow (*anatropi*) of the existing system.[15]

Papandreou's use of the word *overthrow* makes clear that in his eighteenth year he still considered himself something of a revolutionary. However, he was not by any means an admirer of the Soviet Union, and he was shaken by the Moscow purge trials. The Sunday political discussions he continued to have with his father had begun to influence his thinking, as did André Gide. He was reading a great deal in French at this point and later said that Gide's disillusioned account of his return to the Soviet Union in the early '30s had made a deep impression on him.[16] Still searching for the path to an egalitarian world, he turned to Trotskyism, and explained why in his *Pondiki* interview: "Trotskyism, or so it seemed to us, functioned with a certain amount of internal democracy. We embraced it and considered ourselves Trotskyites throughout our school years in Greece. . . . Trotskyism had a certain strength in Greece at that time. It was not what it later became; . . . my friends and I considered ourselves socialists. We didn't want an all-powerful party [or] the harsh dictates of a central authority. Rightly or wrongly, we considered Trotskyism to be true socialism."[17]

The young Trotskyite's dreams to abolish the monarchy and overthrow the social system were considerably dashed on August 4, 1936, when Greece became a dictatorship. Brief but excellent accounts of the developments leading up to the crisis are found in *The Story of Modern Greece*, by C. M. Woodhouse, and *A Short History of Modern Greece*, by Richard Clogg—which I will make briefer here.[18]

The breach between royalists and Venizelists had grown steadily wider during the years of the Second Greek Republic, which was marked by failed coups on both sides until a group of hard-right politicians replaced a moderately conservative prime minster, Panayotis Tsaldaris, with a determined royalist, General George Kondy-lis. Kondylis launched widespread purges of avowed and suspected supporters of Venizelos, who fled into exile and was condemned to death in absentia. (He died of natural causes a year later.) Meanwhile, King George II, having won the 1935 plebiscite by a suspiciously large majority, returned to Greece and ascended to the throne.

As might be expected, the plebiscite and the purges were met with much public unrest. In an effort to restore national harmony the government, with the king's blessing, called for new elections in January 1936. These, however, produced a most inharmonious outcome: a stalemate in which neither royalists nor republicans secured an outright majority and the balance of power was held by the small Popular Front party controlled by the communists. The gravity of the political situation was exacerbated by the economic one: wages plummeted, labor strikes mounted, and the soldiers summoned to quell them often showed more sympathy for the strikers than for the government.

With the country in disarray the king came to rely on his minister of war, General John Metaxas, a strong monarchist (and former coup plotter himself) who advised him to suspend Parliament for five months—a suspension that would last almost ten years. The communists and their allies retaliated by calling a general strike for August 4, 1936. The next day the king issued a proclamation naming Metaxas his new prime minister. This was the event, or train of events, that Andreas Papandreou, opponent of tyranny, whether of the left or the right, saw unfolding in Greece. He was seventeen.

In his book, *Democracy at Gunpoint*, written during his exile, Papandreou recounted his initial reaction. "I remember the morning of August 4, 1936. I had awakened in my Psychiko home and had gone to the outer door for the newspaper. It was not there, so I decided to walk to the square. When I reached it, I found a small crowd gathered in front of a proclamation announcing the coup. I pushed through the crowd, pulled the proclamation off the wall, and tore it to pieces. I was quickly arrested. Later, when I was released from police headquarters, I vowed to work day and night against the regime."[19]

The Past Is Never the Past

This smacks of dramatization, beginning with his opening of the door. There was no home delivery of newspapers; Andreas would have walked to a kiosk anyway, and in peaceful, prosperous Psychiko, it was unlikely there were soldiers poised to arrest him. There is no doubt however that when the character and dimensions of the coup became clear, Papandreou resolved to oppose it with whatever means were available to him. Metaxas's fascist regime would soon neutralize not only the relatively feeble forces of the extreme left but also the more numerous ranks of moderate republicans. Metaxas promptly exiled George Papandreou to the island of Andros and scattered hundreds of other opposition leaders to remote places in Greece.

He also established an efficient internal security apparatus under the direction of Constantine Maniadakis, a skilled operator and veteran of the 1922 Asia Minor campaign. Maniadakis infiltrated the ranks of resistance groups with informers, and Andreas, whose subversive tracts were already on record, was identified as a potential troublemaker.

How much anti-regime work Papandreou undertook at the *peirmatiko scholeio* is unclear. We know how diligently he studied that year, at the same time that he was preparing for entrance examinations to law school. These were highly competitive and must have limited his time to participate in clandestine activities. Again, he placed first among the examinees and entered Athens University's School of Law in the fall of 1937.

From my own later exposure to the leisurely habits of Greek university students I have come to suspect that once in, they have an easier time of it. Attending class seemed to be the least of their concerns and when they did, they slouched in large lecture halls, half listening to a stooped professor reading yellowed notes, which they dutifully regurgitated in their final exams. Such may have been the case with Andreas, who immediately offered his services to EOKDE, a Trotskyite group that opposed both the dictatorship and the orthodox (i.e. Stalinist) Communist Party of Greece, the outlawed KKE.

Papandreou and his first-year law school cohorts were eager workers in EOKDE's cause, but being young, they were given foot soldiers' chores while the higher-ups plotted strategy and tactics. Security was a constant worry, as was competition from rival resistance groups who might trump EOKDE's efforts with operations of their own. Rivals included the Stalinists, moderate conservatives, and even a Venizelist group working on behalf of George Papandreou. (As might have been predicted, all proved ineffectual, and history records no examples of these resistance groups causing any disruption to the Metaxas regime.) Andreas's responsibilities were to mimeograph and distribute EOKDE publications, for which purpose he used an apartment in Athens, possibly his father's, but continued to live with his mother in Psychiko.[20] Meanwhile, the police kept an eye on him, and for a time, a benign one.

The Metaxas regime limited contacts with political exiles, and those hoping to visit them had to fill out cumbersome forms and wait in long lines without any guarantee that their requests would be granted, or even read. Yet on the several occasions Andreas applied for permission to visit his father on Andros, the procedure was expedited by the infamous security director Maniadakis himself. Why? Here we must bear in mind that the Metaxas dictatorship differed from the German and Italian regimes after which it was patterned. Although brutal acts were committed and harsh penalties inflicted on its opponents, the implacably totalitarian character of the Nazi model, and to a lesser extent the Italian Fascist one, was never achieved. In some respects the Metaxas regime was like all Greek governments, democratic or dictatorial, in its quixotic interpretation of the rules.

And so Maniadakis would usher the young Trotskyite into his office, lecture him that his association with EOKDE was well known, and that he would be arrested if it continued. Then he would waive the paperwork, stamp the permit, and wish him a safe journey to Andros. Andreas may have breathed easier. He continued to churn out EOKDE tracts, probably on the assumption that Maniadakis's warnings were pro forma.

He was wrong. In late spring of 1939 Andreas and twelve other dissidents, all friends of his, were arrested and taken to police headquarters. While all were engaged in anti-regime activities, not all

The Past Is Never the Past

were Trotskyites. A student named Cornelios Castoriades, for example, belonged to the Communist Youth Organization of Greece (OKNE) and, although friendly with Andreas, rejected his Trotskyite views as totally heretical.

Whether the thirteen dissidents were arrested at the same time or separately, and what happened to them in custody, are the subject of conflicting accounts. Andreas describes a ghastly ordeal of being beaten to a pulp alternately with psychological interrogation designed to make the prisoner reveal the names of his cohorts.[21] For these methods Andreas gives full credit to Maniadakis's "genius" but is evasive about the extent of his confession. He claims that he was unaware of his friends' arrest until a police officer showed him their names taken from documents seized in his Athens apartment. He says that he later learned that his father, still in exile on Andros, had gotten word to his (male) secretary requesting him to send flowers to a certain lady on her name day.[22] The police, Andreas contends, intercepted the message and, suspecting that it was a coded signal, traced it to the secretary, who was staying in the apartment at the time. There they found the mimeograph machine and the names of subscribers to EOKDE publications.

Michael Macrakis writes that Castoriades, a hardline Stalinist, scoffed at this explanation. It was his belief, shared by some of the other detainees, that Andreas had been arrested before his friends and had surrendered their names to save himself. Castoriades also doubted Andreas's account that he had suffered a broken jaw, suggesting that Andreas was not one to withstand heavy punishment. After all the detainees had been released, several shunned Andreas as a turncoat. To make matters worse, Andreas had signed a statement of repentance for his actions, further tarnishing his standing with EOKDE. The stigma lingered long enough for some hard-left parliamentary deputies to raise questions about the circumstances of his arrest when Andreas ran for office twenty-five years later.

At this distance in time the truth is impossible to determine. Most of the participants in the affair are long dead and the security files were lost or destroyed during World War II and the Greek civil war. It does however seem to be the case that the Nazi occupiers of Greece used the files to identify, and in some cases to execute, individuals whose left-wing sympathies made them likely candidates to join the resistance. Among them were one or two of Andreas's friends, who would probably have been in the files with or without his confession. But as Christina writes in her memoir, she was inclined to believe that under police pressure Andreas had in fact named names and was always remorseful about the consequences. She stops short, however, of saying that he told her this explicitly.[23]

And there the matter must rest. All we know is that Andreas did not return to law school and began to think seriously about leaving Greece. Although he later claimed that he came to this decision reluctantly, prompted by having become a "marked man" and therefore "useless" in the struggle against the dictatorship, others who were also marked, chose to remain.[24] Andreas eulogizes one who paid the ultimate price, his law school mentor, Pandelis Pouliopoulos: "There was, in particular, a man named Pouliopoulos . . . who had learned to combine action with intellect. When the Nazis came, he was summarily executed. . . . Earlier he had refused an offer to recant and leave Greece and he died there as a hero. There was also Versoukis, a tobacco worker and Yannakos, a teacher. Both perished."[25] In these reflections on his youth one senses a certain regret that his own actions had been less than heroic.

Andreas's prudent departure was entirely understandable in a young man of university age, who wanted to live, like countless others, and make his contribution to the world. What is odd is his account of *how* he left Greece, and why he chose to tiptoe around the way it came about. In his *Pondiki* interview, Andreas says that in the spring of 1940 George Papandreou had been released from exile and was living under house arrest in Kastri. Andreas went to consult him about his predicament. After lecturing him that he should have joined his own Venizelist resistance group instead of EOKDE, George Papandreou agreed that it would be wise for Andreas to leave the country, at least temporarily. The problem was that he had no exit visa and was unlikely to obtain one. Once again, we must

The Past Is Never the Past

choose between varying explanations of how Andreas managed to get a temporary document permitting him to travel abroad.

Andreas's version seems farfetched. He claims to have "tricked" Maniadakis into issuing the document by convincing him that his mother, Sophia, had a sister living in the United States and that this sister owed his mother a substantial amount of money. He needed to bring the money back to Greece—and since the country was desperately short of foreign exchange, the director of security agreed to Andreas's request, issuing him a travel document valid for seventeen days. When Andreas arrived in New York he immediately asked for political asylum, citing his imprisonment by the Metaxas regime. On those grounds he was apparently allowed to disembark and given an unlimited residence permit. Was someone, somewhere, also pulling a few strings?

Furthermore, to accept the purpose of Andreas's trip requires us to invest Maniadakis with a degree of naiveté totally at variance with his reputation as a shrewd and cynical security chief who kept voluminous files and had a network of informants. It would have been child's play for Maniadakis to ascertain that Sophia Papandreou had no sister in the United States, much less a sister who owed her a large sum of money.

A more plausible explanation is offered by Michael Macrakis, who believed that Andreas's mother came to his rescue by calling on Maniadakis, reminding him of her father's patriotic actions in the Balkan Wars and pleading mercy for her son. We also know that others in Sophia's circle followed suit. One supplicant who was not a personal friend—but happened to be a patient of Dr. Constantinides, a psychiatrist and the mother of Andreas's Athens College classmate, Paris—was a close relative of Maniadakis, and apparently her intervention as the friend of a friend of a friend persuaded Maniadakis to issue the temporary travel document. In tracking down the story, Macrakis wrote to Paris Constantinides, who confirmed in a letter dated October 13, 1996, "It is true that my mother exerted some influence on Maniadakis . . . through one of her devoted patients . . . a female relative [of Maniadakis]."

There may have been other twists and turns. Like the characters in opéra bouffe, Greek dictators have proven to be generally less omnipotent and more feckless than their historical models. More importantly, they have never lasted very long, and most Greeks take perverse pleasure in ridiculing them. Today, Metaxas is remembered as a tinpot dictator who militarized Boy Scout uniforms and tried to remove the "subversive" funeral oration of Pericles from school textbooks.

At the time, of course, victims of his persecution thought otherwise. Andreas's political predicament was real, as would be his precarious financial situation when he fled Greece. George Papandreou, still under indefinite house arrest and without income from his law practice, warned his son that he could send only one hundred dollars a month. Andreas records that he had fourteen dollars in his pocket when he sailed from Piraeus in early May 1940 aboard the steamship *Nea Ellas*.

Papandreou knew little of the United States: "Only what I studied at Athens College and what I had seen at the cinema."[26] His first inclination had been to go to France where two of his Athens College friends, Romilos Macridis and Peter Sifneos, were already in residence. (After the fall of France both would flee and eventually turn up in America in 1941.) His decision to choose the United States was purely chance, Andreas claimed, based on the suggestion of a friend who was going there.[27] There were probably more pragmatic calculations. War had broken out in Europe the previous September, but neither the United States nor Greece was as yet a belligerent. In addition, Andreas had a useful contact in the United States, an aspiring actress named Aliki Mousouri, Kyveli's daughter from a first marriage, who lived in New York with her lover, the journalist Paul Nord.

Homer Davis had also alerted an Athens College history instructor, Charles Lagoudakis, then fundraising for the college in the United States, to ease Andreas's entry.[28] Lagoudakis was at the pier to greet him when the *Nea Ellas* docked in Hoboken. He then took his protégé to see the Empire State Building, and afterwards to a drugstore for a tuna fish sandwich and a milkshake. Andreas's Americanization had begun.

2

Building a Future

PAPANDREOU'S FIRST INCLINATION was to apply for a scholarship to Columbia University, and with that purpose in mind he moved into its International House on Manhattan's Upper West Side. With little money in his pocket (he had mistakenly squandered much of it at a fashionable barbershop), he supported himself by working as an assistant in the university library and cleaning windows at its Theological School.[1]

Through Lagoudakis and his stepsister, Aliki Mousouri, Andreas was introduced to members of New York's Greek American community, among them Christina Rassia, a recent college graduate with aspirations to enter medical school. Christina lived with her parents and two sisters on the Upper West Side and worked for the renowned biologist, Dr. George Papanicolaou, inventor of the Pap smear test for cancer of the cervix. Within less than a year she would become the first Mrs. Andreas Papandreou. In her memoir Christina, who later became a psychiatrist, describes Andreas at their first encounter as tall and rather shabbily dressed in an ill-fitting greenish tweed suit.[2] Perhaps because of his initial splurge at the pricey barbershop, his hair was long "in the European fashion" with a tendency to stand on end. He reminded her of the comedian Stan Laurel. Nevertheless, she was taken by his charm. Chaperoned by a male cousin, Christina accompanied Andreas to a lecture at International House. She remembers that he lavished compliments on her from the start. When she made a casual joke about not wanting someone to die on her hands, Andreas immediately responded, "What a happy fate, to die in *your* hands!" She was a little shocked, but pleased. They began to see each other regularly.[3]

An innocent abroad he may have been but Papandreou was always a fast learner. By late summer he was instructing newer Greek arrivals about the American way of life, at least as he was living it at Columbia's International House. A younger Athens College alumnus, Paul Mitarachis (who would become a professor of architecture at Yale) recalls how much Andreas seemed at home when he greeted Mitarachis at the pier. He took Paul around lower Manhattan, then up town to 125th Street to show him the wonders of American civilization: a drugstore with food! "Don't call it a pharmacy," Andreas advised, ordering a tuna fish sandwich and a milkshake for him. Then he glanced at the time and apologized that he had to rush off because he had "a date" and was taking her to "the movies."

Reflecting on his initial impression of Andreas as a New York sophisticate, Mitarachis now believes that, like himself, Papandreou was still somewhat naive, particularly about the dating scene, which was nonexistent in Athens College's all male social culture. Andreas was remembered there as very studious, very ambitious, and overtly "political," but not on the lookout for pretty girls. In my conversation with him, Mitarachis said that in all likelihood Andreas had had little time in Greece to socialize with the opposite sex, and that apart from his mother, Christina was probably the first woman with whom he developed a close relationship.[4]

Around the time Papandreou left Mitarachis at the drugstore on 125th Street, Christina writes that she and Andreas were becoming seriously interested in each other. She found him a sparkling conversationalist and attentive listener who valued her opinions and sympathized with her desire to escape her stifling home life. Christina and her sisters had been raised by an excessively closed-minded father (she thought he would have outfitted his daughters with chastity belts had they been available) and a depressed mother who had been hospitalized on several occasions with neurotic ailments.

Christina was awed by Andreas's advanced political views. He was a Trotskyite, he proudly explained, because Trotsky had been the

Building a Future

true leader of the Russian Revolution, whereas Stalin "was only a crude peasant who had betrayed its principles." "From each according to his abilities; to each according to his needs," he quoted Marx knowingly, and she nodded in agreement. How different from her penurious family—and Dr. Papanicolaou, who was paying her a measly forty dollars a month!

Christina's girlfriends were equally charmed by Andreas's sophisticated conversation and elegant manners. When one of them fainted in the street, Andreas rushed to her aid and was so solicitous of her recovery that the young woman told Christina she had never met "so good and considerate a man." As their courtship progressed, Christina began to think that there was something almost saintly about Andreas, and at times she felt "a little unworthy in his company."

Their relationship was extremely chaste. It was only after a month that Andreas ventured a quick kiss, and that in the unromantic setting of Columbus Circle. In response, Christina made the next move and invited him home for lunch. She had seen a recipe in a women's magazine for a concoction called Cheese Dream, made with bacon and tomato along with the feature ingredient, and Andreas was so impressed by her efforts that the next day he presented her with an ode entitled "Cheese Dreams." Christina interpreted his ode as a step toward more than kissing, but all in all, she writes wistfully, their courtship was as innocent as an Andy Hardy movie.[5]

Not long after Christina's Cheese Dream offering, Andreas proposed to her. Christina hesitated to accept. She loved Andreas's qualities and the future he offered beyond her parochial family, but she wasn't sure she was *in* love with him. Another uncertainty was her determination to pursue a career, and she worried that wifely duties would put a stop to that. Andreas was instantly reassuring.

"Christina," she quotes him as saying, "Socialists believe in the equality of the sexes. We will share everything, our work and whatever we have. You can continue your studies after we marry."[6] Then he added the good news that his father intended to raise his financial support to two hundred dollars a month, enough for them to pursue their respective studies without having to work at the same time.

Christina consulted her sisters, her parents, and her friends. Knowing little of Greek politics, she was impressed to learn how prominent the Papandreou name was in Greece. An older friend, a doctor whose judgment she trusted, confirmed the elder Papandreou's renown—and if the son was a chip off the old block, he added with a wink, or perhaps a warning, Andreas would be successful *and* a great lover. Word was that even island exile hadn't dampened George Papandreou's libido, what with fishermen's wives enjoying his company while their husbands spent the day at sea. When Christina repeated this risqué story to Andreas, he said nothing but "smiled enigmatically." On this and subsequent occasions she sensed that Andreas's relations with his father were somewhat strained, in contrast to his mother, whom he idolized. She would soon tire of hearing about Sophia's aristocratic lineage. "At one moment he'd bombard me with Marxist clichés," she wrote, "and the next day about his noble family relations."[7]

The judgment of an ex-spouse should be taken with the usual caveats, but Andreas Papandreou's life was so riddled with inconsistencies that Christina's observations cannot be dismissed as a merely spiteful settling of accounts. In fact her memoir, while by no means flattering to Papandreou, has the marks of a genuine attempt to explain him to herself (more perhaps than to others) and to address the issues that caused their marriage to fail. As a psychiatrist, she tries not to oversimplify them.

After weeks of indecision Christina accepted Andreas's proposal, motivated more by what she was escaping than what she was getting into. Her mother, aunts, and sisters were ecstatic; Christina thought there would have been less excitement in her family if she had written *Gone with the Wind*.[8] Meanwhile, Andreas had changed his mind about attending Columbia, on the advice of a friend who thought Harvard would be a better fit. He applied and was accepted to begin graduate studies in economics in the fall. He moved to Cambridge in mid-September, and from then on, except for occasional weekends, Andreas was separated from Christina until their marriage in February 1941.

Building a Future

Christina and her mother fell to bickering over the wedding arrangements. Mrs. Rassia wanted a lavish ceremony at the Orthodox cathedral at Fifth Avenue and Seventy-Third Street; Christina, a simpler one. Andreas tried to mediate between them without indicating his own preference. When her mother's wishes prevailed, however, he outdid Mrs. Rassia by asking Archbishop Athanagoras of North and South America to officiate. The archbishop declined (for political reasons, Christina thought), and Andreas angrily told her that Athanagoras would regret his decision when George Papandreou returned to politics. This return being unlikely to occur in 1941, Andreas (and Christina's mother) had to settle for a local priest to preside over the nuptials.[9]

Throughout their engagement Andreas continued to behave toward Christina with great propriety. Christina was eager for more intimate relations, but Papandreou told her gravely that in his opinion a young woman should remain a virgin until she was married. He assured her that the wait would be worthwhile. "You can't imagine, Christina, what rapture awaits you," she quotes him as telling her. This of course only increased her impatience and frustration. The reality, which she experienced only six months after their marriage, failed to live up to his predictions.[10] (Some forty years later her disappointment would resemble how, for politically virginal members of the Greek left, Andreas's promises to overthrow Greece's entire social system would also become a rapture indefinitely deferred.)

Shortly after her engagement Christina received a warm letter from Andreas's mother welcoming her into the family, saying she had placed her future daughter-in-law's picture next to her bed to look at each morning when she awakened. Christina responded in Greek, but used Latin letters because although she spoke the language, she had never learned to write in it. Sophia seemed to have been touched by her effort. Christina makes no mention of a welcome letter from George Papandreou, still under house arrest in Kastri; nor does she seem concerned that the Germans were about to invade Greece.

Between visits the couple wrote to each other and in one letter Christina enclosed a poem she had composed as a college student entitled, "For Emily Dickinson." Andreas replied brusquely, "I am reminded that with the world ready for the Revolution, we should not waste our time on melancholy poetesses."[11]

Papandreou's reading at that time was primarily dedicated to his studies, but Christina remembers him remarking, as they were strolling on Riverside Drive in New York, that he considered Victor Hugo's *Les Miserables* the most important social novel ever written. His admiration for Hugo, the great writer, social critic, and lover, led Christina to think that he saw much of his father in the author. Although more familiar with French literature than American or English, Andreas gave Christina Hemingway's *For Whom the Bell Tolls* just after it was published. She had never been able to afford hardcover books and was so proud of her gift that she displayed it like an engagement ring, reading it on park benches and city buses, to honor the man she was about to marry.[12]

As winter set in Papandreou had yet to settle on his best man, or *koumbaros*, a role that assumes significant, usually lifelong, responsibilities in the Orthodox religion. His choice was an unusual one. Perhaps out of indebtedness (or on socialist principle) he approached Peter Queen, a Greek American fruit and vegetable wholesaler in Cambridge. Queen had offered Andreas temporary lodging in his household, which included an overweight wife and two equally rotund daughters. Andreas moved in, but soon complained to Christina that Mrs. Queen was lazy and treated her husband disrespectfully. His disapproval notwithstanding, he invited Peter to be his best man, and the Queen family excitedly made plans for the big day in New York, now set for February 7, 1941.

For her part, Christina was pleased to note improvements in her fiancé's appearance. Andreas had curbed his appetite for milk shakes, slimmed down, and cut his hair short. He had even bought a new suit, overcoat, and hat. He had also grown overly fastidious, as Christina noticed when they visited a young married couple making do in a cramped Boston apartment. Andreas used the bathroom and was appalled that it also served as a kitchenette, with vegetables by the sink and underwear hanging from the doorknob—never mind that the husband was a medical intern as impecunious as he. Toward Christina he showed the same duality, treating her in public as a liberated American woman and in private as a virginal Greek girl "whose chastity would be proved after the wedding night by holding up the bed sheets for display."[13]

Then Peter Queen began to get cold feet. He feared that the elder Papandreou would expect someone more distinguished than he to be his son's *koumbaros*. Andreas continued to insist that, as socialists, both his father and he cared little for a man's position or background. But Peter Queen held his ground, and Andreas had to replace him at the last minute with a New York ophthalmologist whom the bridal couple knew only in passing.

Christina does not describe the ceremony, only that she and Andreas spent their wedding night at the Lexington Hotel, where Andreas promptly fell asleep and she lay awake listening to the traffic. They then spent a frugal weekend honeymoon at the Pickwick Arms Hotel in Greenwich, Connecticut, which was equally anticlimactic. "We lay with our arms around each other like lost children," Christina writes sadly. Despite her vastly disappointing introduction to married life, when the couple returned to New York to have dinner with her parents Andreas confessed that after such "intimacy" he felt "strange" confronting her father.[14] The next morning Andreas and Christina left for Cambridge. As the train pulled out of the station her mother called out last minute instructions on how to cook roast lamb. It was useful advice, she writes, but hardly pertinent to the situation.

The newlyweds found a small semi-furnished apartment at 16 Chauncey Street and almost immediately faced money problems when the monthly checks from George Papandreou turned out to be not two, but one hundred dollars, the maximum amount he was allowed to send out of the country. The sum was far too small to cover expenses, causing great anxiety in Christina if somewhat less so in Andreas, who throughout his life took money more seriously in theory than in practice.

And with each passing month her vision of a marriage between equals receded along with her hopes of entering medical school. Deeply absorbed in his studies, Andreas became oblivious to her presence. Christina remembers him pacing the floor in the middle of the night, lost in thought, then suddenly calling out to her "Christina, I have just solved a complicated problem!" or "I have just had an interesting idea!" Those ideas never paid the rent. To augment their income, when Christina's sister Maria found a job in Cambridge and rented a room near Chauncey Street, she agreed to take her evening meals with the Papandreous and pay fifty cents to do so.

Soon there were more mouths to feed. Throughout 1941 a stream of Greek students fled Europe for the United States, many ending up in Cambridge. Two of them were Andreas's aforementioned classmates Romilos (Roy) Macridis and Peter Siphneos, who had made their way out of France and eventually to Harvard, to finish their respective studies in political science and medicine. When they arrived in Cambridge, they rented a room in the same building as Maria, and Christina found herself stretching the meals for them as well.

One can imagine the camaraderie that was reignited by their reunion. The three fell into long discussions together, speaking in French, which Christina had studied but could not follow easily. To improve her comprehension she asked Andreas to converse in French with her, but he derided the idea. "In the United States French is a language for snobs," he said, as if she'd be putting on airs by speaking it.[15] Increasingly, she was relegated to the kitchen while the three schoolboy chums laughed and argued until one night the landlord appeared to complain about the noise. This led to a heated exchange that ended with the Papandreous' eviction. Christina, who worried about keeping up appearances, was sure that the real cause for the landlord's action was not the noise but the fact that they "exuded poverty."[16] Fortunately, they found an affordable apartment nearby at 26 Concord Avenue, with a washer and dryer as well as a less irascible landlord.

Shortly after they settled in, Macridis and Siphneos moved into an apartment across the hall. Their presence was soon augmented by the arrival of more Greek students, clustering together as exiles do in new surroundings and forming their own *parea*, or "circle," as we would say. But for all Greeks, and particularly upper-middle-class Greeks, a *parea* is deeper and longer lasting than a group of friends one hangs out with for a time and may outgrow in later life.[17] In that respect a *parea* is like an English club, its members conjoined by similar backgrounds, education, and tastes; in another it is an extended Greek family, intrusive, and utterly lacking the Anglo-Saxon's sense of privacy. The late British travel writer, Robert Liddell, was devoted to the Greeks but was also a fussy bachelor who suffered their constant presence when he stayed with them. "No one will ever ask if you would like to retire to your room to write letters," he warned his readers. So it was for Christina in Andreas's *parea*, which she felt was like living on the fringes of a clan that she would never be asked to join.

Between food and finances Christina turned her thoughts toward finding a job. In low moments she considered leaving Andreas but feared the social consequences. The Rassias lived by the code of the Greek village and considered divorce a dishonor to the whole family. Her mother was inordinately proud of her daughter's marriage, and her father's only advice to Christina was "to be a good Greek wife." She chose to stay on but still resented her subservient role after a courtship that had promised equality and independence. In the meantime, Andreas completed his studies in a record three years, receiving his master's in a year and his PhD in economics in 1943. Christina typed his thesis but found the 350-page double-spaced manuscript somewhat "tedious."

By then Andreas had learned to separate his personal from his academic life, his politics from his studies. His Harvard professors regarded him as a gifted student who in a remarkably short period had mastered the pragmatic American approach to economics and discarded what was foreign to it, such as the habit of European academics to view capitalist economies through a political lens. They would have been surprised to learn of his Trotskyite beliefs and interest in social engineering as a path to a better world. Professor

Sydney Alexander, who knew the Papandreous at Harvard immediately after the war, thought that Andreas was far more interested in strengthening capitalism than hastening its demise.

His choice of courses and the professors whose intellectual influence is most visible in his written work at Harvard reveal the same shift in perspective. The onset of the Great Depression a decade earlier had brought new urgency to the field. How to encourage growth, maximize employment, and define the proper relationship of the state to private enterprise were problems of immediate as well as theoretical importance. In the 1940s Harvard's most eminent economist was the Moravian-born Joseph Schumpeter, whose inquiries into capital development, business cycles, and the role of the entrepreneur had produced works that were already mainstream economics classics. At the other end of the spectrum the Soviet experiment (and the apparently unending crisis of capitalism) was still taught by a minority of Marxist professors; meanwhile, a third school of thought taking hold at Harvard was led by the Keynesian disciple, Professor Alvin Hansen. Given his background, one might suppose that Andreas would be drawn to the Marxist courses, or to the freshness and intellectual complexity of Keynesian economics. Neither seems to have been the case.

Michael Macrakis investigated the economics courses Papandreou took between 1940 and 1943.[18] None were in Marxist theory or practice, and if he was exposed to Keynesian thought in an introductory course he did not venture further on his own. Andreas's thesis advisor, Professor William L. Crum, was a mathematical and statistical analyst and a close collaborator of Joseph Schumpeter's. While we cannot be certain what direct contact there may have been between Schumpeter and Papandreou, we can be sure that the older man's work was central to Andreas's choice of subject matter for his dissertation. It is probable as well that Papandreou was influenced by the chairman of the economics department who at that time was Professor Edward H. Chamberlin, a champion of private enterprise and critic of state intervention in the economy.

In selecting an area of research for his dissertation Papandreou avoided the entire field of state economic policy and chose instead to investigate the nature and process of decision-making in American private enterprise. It was an unusual choice for a foreign graduate student who had been in the United States little more than two years and had no personal or family experience in private sector management. In later years Papandreou told his *Pondiki* interviewer that researching where the decision-making authority lay in two hundred leading American corporations was extremely difficult, requiring him to learn who was who in corporate America, along with statistical data.[19] He did not, however, explain why he chose the topic. He might have decided to stay within the mainstream of Harvard's economic thinking at the time or simply to explore a field of economics that was new to him. Christina always believed that Andreas had chosen the subject to conceal his true political convictions. As is often the case with Papandreou, when there are several explanations for his behavior, all are probably in some degree correct.

Andreas submitted "The Location and Scope of the Entrepreneurial Function, with Particular Emphasis on Corporate Developments" on September 3, 1943. The dissertation is a dense study of the characteristics of entrepreneurial decision-making, the relationship of management to ownership, and an estimation of whether true entrepreneurs can exist in differing types of economies. In an interesting final section, which he acknowledges is speculative, he estimates how the "entrepreneurial function" might evolve after the end of World War II in conjunction with state-managed economies. This is the only part of the thesis that reveals his underlying thoughts about the feasibility of the state assuming the role of entrepreneur.

To judge from references and quotations in the dissertation, a seminal influence on Papandreou's thinking (and probably also on his choice of subject) was a ground-breaking work by Adolph A. Berle and Gardiner C. Means that analyzed the legal implications of corporate growth and the structural transformation of corporations that accompanied it.[20] The study, first published in 1932, was reissued in 1939, a year before Papandreou arrived in the United States. Berle was a lawyer by training and his collaboration with the economist Means opened up a new field of scholarly research. Until then, economists and legislators had focused more on the antitrust implications of corporate growth than on the internal mechanics of corporations or the significance of changes in the relationship between owners and managers. Berle's celebrity as an early member of the Roosevelt administration's Brain Trust and his subsequent break with administration policy in the midthirties added to the attention the book received.

A principle point that Berle and Means made in their book was that the increasing size of corporations and the complexity of managing them had distanced owners (i.e., the entrepreneurs) from managers, with the result that managers were now becoming entrepreneurs themselves. For Berle and Means, as for Schumpeter, the true entrepreneur was a corporate leader who played a creative or innovative role. Papandreou defined this as "the making of profit-maximizing decisions whose outcome is dependent on the unregulated forces of the economy."[21] Since the ability to make profitable decisions in conditions of uncertainty was a condition of true entrepreneurship, Papandreou concluded that it could not exist in a communist economy. In a fully *regulated* capitalist economy, however, he argued that the state could perform the function of entrepreneur, since it "would be partly engaged in the effort to keep up the profitability of investment at large."[22] Perhaps to disabuse his readers of any notion that he foresaw or favored the emergence of fully regulated capitalist economies, Papandreou appended a footnote to this section of the thesis: "It will be obvious to the reader that this is an extreme case, which is conceivable analytically but may not find historical counterparts. It is discussed only for the purpose of making clear the implications of my definition of entrepreneurship."[23]

But Papandreou seems to have had more in mind than a theoretical model. Somewhere in his reading and research the image of the entrepreneur as a leadership figure—indeed a national leadership figure—must have captured his imagination. This idea of the state as entrepreneur in a fully regulated economy allowed him to indulge his admiration for captains of industry without abandoning his socialist principles and distrust of untrammeled capitalism. His description of the concept is revealing. "What would have changed in a case like this is the location of that [entrepreneurial] function and its scope, but the function itself would not disappear. On the contrary, it would gain a new glamour [*sic*] and a new significance.... The entrepreneur in this case would be the state. The unit would be the nation, the nation as a whole engaged in a national enterprise of impressive dimensions."[24]

In his analysis of where decision-making authority lay, Papandreou concluded that of two hundred leading non-financial corporations in the United States, in only one-eighth did entrepreneurship coincide with ownership. In all the other cases the true entrepreneurs were the managers. This distancing of management from ownership, which he believed would continue to expand, created a vacuum that the state could fill. The vision of the state as entrepreneur, coping with a multitude of variable factors in the world economy, making innovative decisions that encouraged national growth and avoided the stultifying effects of state management that were all too apparent in the Soviet Union, may explain the intense interest that Papandreou showed later on in the Yugoslav economy. Unfortunately, that model, which purported to introduce elements of internal competition into a state-run economy, proved as calamitous as its Soviet progenitor. If the state can succeed as an entrepreneur in the sense envisioned by Papandreou, none has yet managed to do so.

Most economists at this time agreed that the role of entrepreneur would continue to change after World War II. Berle and Means had outlined four possible courses of development, of which assumption by the state of entrepreneurial function was only one. Papandreou made a bolder prediction, which is succinctly summarized in the abstract of his thesis that precedes the full text: "With respect to postwar developments, an increasing significance of state entrepreneurial activity is predicted as compared to private entrepreneurship. In this pattern of change the separation of the 'ownership' and the 'entrepreneur' function paves the way for the final shift in the location of the entrepreneurial function from the private to the public sphere."[25]

When Papandreou's dissertation is read from this standpoint, from back to front, as it were, his own predilections are fairly clear and Christina's surmise that he had chosen the topic of private sector entrepreneurship to conceal them becomes more convincing. His personal views are presented discreetly, even artfully, in the context and language of mainstream economic theory. But there is nothing in the dissertation to contradict his youthful conviction that unregulated market economies had plunged the world into economic crisis and that increasing management of national economies by the state was inevitable if the world was to emerge from the crisis.

At home, the Papandreous' own financial crisis continued to plague their marriage. At one point, money was so scarce that Andreas went to New York to ask Spyros Skouras, the president of Twentieth Century Fox and an acquaintance of his father, if he could find a way for his father to send more than a hundred dollars a month. The film mogul proved unhelpful, and when Christina's sister, Maria, moved to Rochester, reducing the couple's income by fifty cents a day, Christina took a job.

After working for short periods at the Harvard Coop and the university employment office at the prevailing rate of thirty-five cents an hour, she found better pay and shorter hours doing secretarial work for the revered emeritus professor of English, Charles Townsend Copeland. Copey, as he was affectionately known, was a Harvard legend whose undergraduate students had included Franklin Roosevelt and John Reed. Now in his late eighties, Professor Copeland had a clear mind but a failing memory, and one of Christina's duties was to keep him from writing letters to friends and former students already deceased. Christina became devoted to her kind and dignified employer, who called her "Mrs. Papan" and provided a more congenial atmosphere in his study than the one that awaited her at home.

She was discovering that Andreas, like his father, had a volcanic temper beneath the amiable exterior he displayed to the outside world. He could also be jealous, as she found out on one occasion when she spent a day at Andover with a male friend she had known in New York. The relationship was purely platonic, she had Andreas's permission to go, and the friend was accompanied by a teacher at Phillips Andover Academy. Although she was home before dark and had been suitably chaperoned, she returned an hour or so later than planned and Andreas immediately accused her of having a wandering eye. In a strange transfer of authority, Andreas told her, "My father would never allow you to make a fool of me." The next day he was still so incensed that he took the friend's wedding present to them, a leather-bound edition of Walt Whitman's *Leaves of Grass*, and sold it to a second-hand bookshop. "This book can no longer remain in our house," he lectured her, "my father would never permit it."[26]

If this recollection is accurate, it indicates Andreas's severe lack of confidence in his own sexual prowess. In the course of researching this memoir, I was told by a critic of Christina's that she was frigid, pointing out that she remained childless while Andreas would produce four children with his second wife, Margaret. Christina makes several references to her sexual life but in the context of an unconsummated honeymoon and the absence of marital relations for six months thereafter. Whatever hampered them both, Andreas obviously felt the need to keep up his self-esteem, apparently through his father. His behavior typifies the Greek term *filotimo*, which Greeks define as "love of honor," that is, the responsibility to assert one's dignity when faced with the possibility of losing it. *Filotimo* often strikes outsiders as no more than nasty pride, brandished like a flag to disguise personal failings. As he adapted himself to American ways, Andreas was outwardly easy-going, but when his Greek sensibilities were ruffled his *filotimo* was never far from the surface. He took umbrage when his male prerogatives were overlooked, however innocently, even by Christina's anxious-to-please mother. She once neglected to keep a slice of *vasilopita*, the traditional New Year's Eve bread, for his breakfast the next morning. "At my house," he said churlishly, "my mother always woke me with a piece of *vasilopita*."[27]

To her litany of complaints, Christina adds Andreas's tendency to hold a grudge against political opponents, even into the next generation. He refused to socialize with a Greek medical student, a personable young man and fellow refugee, because he was the son of a former Athens mayor during the Metaxas regime. Christina thought it a vindictive snub, since the Metaxas regime, after heroic resistance, had already succumbed to the Germans.[28] This unforgiving character trait would remain with Andreas all his life and assume greater significance when he tired of academic politics in the United States and took up the real thing in Greece.

For all the nights he debated with his *parea* the fateful decade in Europe that led up to World War II, Andreas seemed to ignore the implications of the war for the United States. He had entered Harvard in the midst of the 1940 presidential campaign, in which a dominant issue was whether the military successes of the Axis powers would ultimately imperil the security of the United States. The debates between isolationists and interventionists continued until Pearl Harbor, but Andreas's thoughts seemed to have focused on getting his degree and a job that would get him started in the economics field. In 1942, while still writing his doctorate, he managed to secure a part-time lectureship at Boston College, a Catholic institution in the suburb of Newton, and during the same academic year, 1942–43, he also became a part-time teaching fellow at Harvard.

Between classes and two jobs Andreas may have had little time to follow world events, but then like other Trotskyites—indeed like Trotsky himself—he may have looked on the war as a contest between two doomed and equally complicit imperialisms. One recalls in this connection Andreas's disdain for the idea of reading Emily Dickinson when the world was "ready for the Revolution." The letter in which he expressed those sentiments would have been in the fall or early winter of 1940 after the fall of France and probably after Italy's attack on Greece. For Trotskyites, of course, this indifference would have continued even after Hitler's invasion of the Soviet Union in June 1941, an event that instantly converted orthodox Stalinists from apostles of non-engagement into ardent interventionists.

Detached observers the Trotskyites may have believed themselves to be, but the war was beginning to affect the lives of everyone in the United States. As a resident alien Papandreou was subject to the draft, and in the spring or summer of 1943 he considered enlisting in

Building a Future

the United States Navy. (The decision may have reflected his third career choice on the experimental school questionnaire, or simply the tradition of educated Greek men to pick the more elitist navy over the army.) Perhaps more for domestic reasons than patriotic ones, he enlisted that fall, after receiving his PhD, and shortly after was sent for basic training to Great Lakes Naval Training Station in Illinois.

With Andreas away, and more money in the bank from his teaching salaries (and later his military pay), Christina's situation began to improve. She enrolled at Boston University Medical School simultaneously with Andreas's departure for Illinois. After the doubts, frustrations, and penuries of the previous two and a half years Christina believed she was at last headed toward a career. But the life she had once envisioned with Andreas was falling apart, and despite one or two furloughs with him that briefly rekindled their affection for each other, they became further estranged when Andreas was offered an assistant professorship at the University of Minnesota and Christina stayed behind to finish her medical degree.

Andreas remained at Great Lakes for at least six months. His basic training lasted nine to twelve weeks, after which he spent another fifteen weeks at the Hospital Corps School to qualify as a navy corpsman.[29] Christina notes that his first furlough coincided with the break between her first and second six-month semesters at medical school, placing it in about March 1944. From Great Lakes Andreas was subsequently assigned as a pharmacist's mate to Geneva, New York, then to Bethesda Naval Hospital, just outside of Washington DC, and finally to Mare Island outside San Francisco.

Our knowledge of Papandreou's duties as a navy corpsman is sketchy. *Pondiki* reports that he studied tropical diseases at Bethesda Naval Hospital.[30] At Mare Island his duties changed by a stroke of luck. According to his second son, Nick Papandreou, Andreas was hitchhiking back to base after a weekend liberty in San Francisco and was picked up by an admiral.[31] When the admiral discovered that the pharmacist's mate had a PhD in economics from Harvard, he arranged for Andreas's speedy transfer to a statistical control unit planning for the Okinawa invasion. This major amphibious landing, launched on April 1, 1945, was one of the bloodiest in the Pacific War, lasting two months and incurring forty-eight thousand American casualties. In all likelihood, Andreas's statistical work at Mare Island dealt with forecasting casualties and supplies needed for the dead and wounded.

The sailor's life, if not at sea, seems to have suited Andreas. Christina found him relaxed and physically fit on his first furlough in Boston. On a later reunion in Bethesda the couple took in all the Washington sights, standing "awestruck" before the Lincoln Memorial and reverently reading the inscriptions on the newly completed Jefferson Memorial: "I have sworn upon the altar of God eternal hostility against every form of tyranny over the mind of man."[32] Fortified by their brisk walks around the nation's capital, they went on to dine and dance at the Statler hotel.

In July 1944 Christina enjoyed another weekend excursion with Andreas when he was invited to attend the Bretton Woods Conference, the historic international gathering of statesmen and economists who would set the new rules for the postwar international monetary system. The invitation was arranged by George Papandreou, then living in Cairo, and Winston Churchill's newly appointed prime minister of the Greek government-in-exile. The reasoning behind Churchill's choice had to do with the ongoing guerrilla war between nationalists and communists on the Greek mainland, which the British hoped to pacify—or at least paper over—by promising both factions a leader who was neither a monarchist nor a communist and who would unite the country after the war, the end of it now in sight. And the reasoning behind George Papandreou's choice of his own son as a participant at the Bretton Woods Conference was his hope that it would lead him to some sort of international position in Greece. Andreas rejected the idea. He had already applied for American citizenship, which was quickly granted to foreigners who had served in the armed forces, and made clear to his father that he intended to pursue a career in the United States.

3

Personal and Postwar Developments

THE LEADING PROPONENT of the Bretton Woods Conference and a dominant figure during its deliberations was the eminent British economist John Maynard Keynes. Delegates from forty-four nations participated in the conference, for which the United States and Great Britain had largely set the agenda in advance. As a member of the Greek delegation, Andreas would have played a minor role, perhaps as translator, and what he thought of the conference's achievements, among them the creation of the World Bank and the International Monetary Fund, is not recorded in his writings or in Christina's memoir. More interested in the setting than the subject of the conference, she describes the luxurious accommodations of the Mount Washington Hotel in New Hampshire ("where wealthy couples spent their summers accompanied by nursemaids and chauffeurs") and the sight of Lord Keynes, enfeebled by heart disease, walking on the arm of his wife. Christina nourished a fantasy that he would have a heart attack during the conference and that she would be summoned in the middle of the night to save him. (Keynes survived his stay but died two years later.) Christina had to leave early for medical school courses, and she recalls meeting Andreas in the bar for a farewell drink. "A really good scotch," she notes with satisfaction before they parted again.[1]

Some ten months later, in late April 1945, Andreas was again on the Greek delegation at the founding conference of the United Nations in San Francisco. The charter had been drafted at Dumbarton Oaks the previous year by the Big Four—the United States,

Great Britain, the Soviet Union, and China—and there were now fifty-one nations represented. Its liberation and George Papandreou's return notwithstanding, Greece was represented by a nonpolitical service government of no consequence. Although in January 1945, a truce had ended street fighting in Athens, the elder Papandreou had already resigned his premiership in December 1944. Still, he may have put in a good word for his son, and because Andreas was stationed in the San Francisco area he was probably called upon again for translating services, as Nick Papandreou believes.[2]

The war was drawing to an end and, with it, Andreas's military service. His newly acquired American citizenship did not annul his Greek one (anyone with a paternal Greek grandfather never loses his Greek citizenship), and had Andreas considered putting his skills to work in his ravaged homeland, even temporarily, there was much that a Harvard-trained economist with a prominent name could do to help.[3] That said, I find it quite understandable that he would choose to stay where he was; most young Greeks living abroad did the same, at a time when Greece was virtually a failed state. Furthermore, it was a time that Andreas clearly wanted to distance himself from his father. In 1946 his marriage was in limbo, and his career looked anything but promising.

He fretted that his two-year absence from Harvard had hampered his chances to be invited back as a member of the faculty. Christina reports that shortly before his discharge Andreas sent her a copy of a letter that he had written to Harvard economists who had not done military service, reminding them that while he had been in the navy they had been free to climb farther up Harvard's professional ladder. Christina was embarrassed by the letter's tone of entitlement, but in fact Andreas's concerns were not unfounded.[4] He was offered a lowly position as an instructor in economics and then assigned with several other junior instructors to teach a basic course, Principles of Economics, and one other course, Public Enterprise and Control in Transport, Communications, and Utilities. The course closest to his dissertation and continuing interest, the Corporation and its Regulation, was taught by his former thesis advisor, Professor Crum, in conjunction with Assistant Professor Stanley Alexander. Alexander had received his PhD in economics three years after Andreas but had worked during the war in the Office of Strategic Services, thereby gaining an edge on Andreas in practical economics as well as a higher academic rank. Michael Macrakis diligently read Alexander's thesis on the financial structure of American corporations since 1890 and found it superior to Papandreou's, most likely due, he concluded, to Alexander's direct involvement in government economic planning before embarking on his own dissertation.[5] Macrakis also notes that Papandreou's office in the academic year 1946–47 was in Winthrop House, where Andreas was a student advisor, rather than in the prestigious Littauer Building, where the economics department and Alexander's office were located.[6]

Andreas grew more frustrated when he was not promoted to assistant professor in 1947, with the explanation that instructors had to wait three years before becoming eligible. "I don't know if I can stand two more years of this!" he told Christina.[7] He began to explore openings at other universities. Harvard's 1946–47 course catalog lists Papandreou as an instructor in economics "through September 30, 1947," suggesting that he had committed himself only until then or, alternatively, that Harvard was hiring him on a year-to-year contract.[8] In May 1947, he was offered a job at the University of Buffalo. After sitting up most of a night discussing the pros and cons, with Christina arguing that it would be a professional dead end, Andreas declined the offer.

He continued building a network of contacts, both in the academic world and in the Greek American community. Meanwhile, Christina graduated from medical school in the late spring of 1947 but still had to do a year's internship in Boston when the University of Minnesota offered Andreas a position as assistant professor in its economics department.[9] Andreas accepted the job eagerly; Christina worried about the long separation it would entail until she could join him the following summer. She was pleased for his sake but also well aware that her husband of six years had never learned to fold his socks, much less wash them.

Not surprisingly, Andreas's mother offered a practical and emotionally satisfying solution for Andreas, who may have had the idea all along. She would come to the United States to live with him during Christina's absence. Andreas left promptly for Minneapolis before Sophia's arrival, leaving Christina to meet and house her mother-in-law until Andreas found a place to live. Both women were nervous about their first encounter. Christina describes Sophia Papandreou as a "small, round woman with a sweet face who appeared older than her years" and "as apprehensive as if she were going to the guillotine instead of to be reunited with her beloved son."[10] The time they would spend together, both in Cambridge and Minneapolis, was one of courteous incomprehension. Aside from the usual adjustments called for when a mother and daughter-in-law live under the same roof, Christina was determinedly agnostic and Sophia deeply pious. She prayed many times a day not only for the protection of those she loved but, as Andreas enigmatically explained later to Christina, "for the destruction of her enemies."[11]

Until Andreas received his first paycheck from the University of Minnesota, Christina had to budget fiercely, even borrowing several hundred dollars from a friend to tide her over until she could join Andreas in the summer of 1948. He would, however, be making a respectable $4,500 a year—enough, his mother happily assumed, for the couple to start a family and for her services to continue.

This was a delicate subject that Christina avoids in her book, or rather sublimates by focusing on her personal struggles to pay the bills, finish medical school, and cope with a difficult husband. There may have been physical problems or sexual incompatibility that made pregnancy unlikely. Whatever the cause, the three years that Christina spent in Minneapolis, periodically returning to the East Coast, were humiliating and fruitless. She chafed at living in a ménage à trois, and even after Sophia arranged to sleep at night at a next door neighbor's house "her diminutive but determined figure" appeared bright and early each morning to pat her daughter-in-law's stomach and ask, "Is the baby there yet?" She needn't have bothered. Christina's successor was already on the scene.

1. Andreas Papandreou with the author and his wife, circa 1960. Courtesy of Margaret Papandreou and the Andreas G. Papandreou Foundation.

2. Three generations of Greek prime ministers: Grandfather George Papandreou, son Andreas, and grandson George, circa 1960. *New York Times*, July 12, 2011.

3. Andreas and Margaret Papandreou and their children in Canada, circa 1971. Courtesy of the Andreas G. Papandreou Foundation.

4. Andreas greeted by enthusiastic crowds after his return to Athens from exile, 1974. Courtesy of the Athens *Kathimerini* Newspaper Archives.

5. Now that he is the avowedly anti-American leader of Greece's first socialist party, PASOK, Andreas's rising star brings him to . . . Author's collection.

6. . . . the premiership in the 1981 elections. Here he is received by Constantine Karamanlis, president of the Hellenic Republic.
Courtesy of the Athens *Kathimerini* Newspaper Archives.

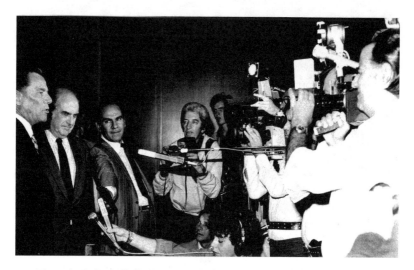

7. The author's first call on the newly elected prime minister causes a media frenzy.
Author's collection.

8. Old acquaintances, however, manage a friendly handshake. Author's collection.

9. Presentation of credentials to President Karamanlis (who would be ousted by PASOK in 1984). Author's collection.

10. PASOK Minister of culture, famed actress, and passionate advocate for the return of the Elgin Marbles to Greece Melina Mercouri, between the author and his wife, 1983. Author's collection.

11. End of an Era: An ailing Papandreou and an aging Karamanlis, Greece's most dominant post–World War II political leaders, and rivals, 1994. Courtesy of the Athens *Kathimerini* Newspaper Archives.

4

Romance and Return

MARGARET CHANT HAD graduated from the University of Minnesota in 1946 with a degree in journalism. She was the eldest of five daughters, raised in a working-class family from Elmhurst, Illinois, a Chicago suburb. A striking twenty-four-year-old with long legs, russet hair, and confident demeanor, her progressive political views would spark Andreas's dormant ones but were more pragmatic than theoretical. Margaret had worked her way through university, then stayed on in Minneapolis, trying to make a go of a one-woman public relations business.

They met in February 1948, in the waiting room of a Greek Cypriot dentist who had enlisted Margaret to help him write a memoir in exchange for free dental treatment. "A tooth per chapter," as she put it. Margaret began the conversation as she was pondering how to smarten up a magazine advertisement she was working on, and because Andreas "looked vaguely foreign," she asked if he could translate a phrase for her into French. The conversation led to dinner, and dinner led to an affair. Like Christina, Margaret was quickly dazzled by Andreas's charm, worldliness, and intellectual gifts; he, in turn, was attracted to her midwestern populism as well as by her looks. Through Margaret, Andreas would join Minnesota's Democratic Reform Party and become acquainted with its notables, future Democratic Party vice president Hubert Humphrey and future Minnesota governor Orville Freeman. Twenty years later, both men would be instrumental in securing Andreas's release from prison.

The Cypriot dentist had entitled his memoir *Thrice a Stranger*, having moved three times between his homeland and the United States, each time discovering that he had become a stranger in both. When Margaret explained the title to Andreas he laughed and said that he had no such problem. "He felt nostalgia for Greece," she writes, "but no desire to return."[1]

Andreas wasted no time consummating the courtship. Perhaps for the first time in his life he was truly, passionately in love, and in the spring of 1948, two months before Christina's arrival from Cambridge, he confessed the fact in a letter to her and asked her to grant him a divorce. Despite the years of tensions in their marriage, Christina writes that the letter came as an unexpected blow. With her father's injunction to be a "good Greek wife," she still felt an obligation to join him in Minnesota, to try again, and perhaps at some point produce an heir.

Along with Sophia's efforts, this obligation had been made clear to her over the previous Christmas when George Papandreou's estranged wife, the actress Kyveli, visited New York to look into schools for their son, George.[2] Andreas and Christina, also in New York to visit the Rassias, spent an evening with her, during which Kyveli sized up Christina and didn't like what she saw. "I gave up my *whole* career for George Papandreou and motherhood," she chastised Christina for wanting to have a career of her own. This was hardly the case; Kyveli remained first lady of the stage for many years after bearing her son but being both Greek and an actress she threw herself into the role of a humble wife. "You seem to think you've married a chauffeur, not a Papandreou," she snapped at her step daughter-in-law. Christina, embarrassed and infuriated, looked to Andreas to come to her defense, but as he did with his father, he remained silent, smiling his "enigmatic" smile.[3]

Unhappy as she was, but not yet prepared to face the future alone, Christina flew to Minneapolis to salvage what was left of their marriage. A grim-faced Andreas met her at the airport and for the next twenty-four hours tried to explain to Christina that he would always love her but had found in Margaret a true soul mate that neither of them would find in each other. Christina sensed that Margaret had

also fallen for Andreas's courtship spiel about marital and professional equality between the sexes, and that proved to be the case—at
least after Margaret had done her duty to have children. Certainly,
as Andreas rose in Greek politics, Margaret campaigned vigorously
to include women's rights in PASOK's platform and is justly credited as the driving force behind the many Greek laws that guarantee
them today. But also like Christina, her belief in an equal partner-
ship with Andreas led to a rift, and eventual divorce.[4]

Less assertive than Margaret, Christina spent her brief encounter with Andreas avoiding confrontation by persuading him to discuss his dilemma with a psychiatrist. She never learned exactly what
exchanges took place between them, but they had the desired effect.
With his customary ambivalence, Andreas agreed to give the marriage another try.[5]

Christina moved to Minneapolis and for another three years clung
miserably to her marriage. Margaret meanwhile fled Minnesota and
applied to several graduate schools to earn a degree as a medical
social worker. When she was accepted only by her alma mater, and
only with financial help from Minnesota's Public Health Service, she
returned to Minneapolis in 1949. She avoided running into Andreas
until the spring of 1950 by which time, most likely on the rebound,
she was engaged to a fellow graduate student whom she married in
July and then moved with him to California. Their respective mar-
riages notwithstanding, and still drawn to each other, Andreas and
Margaret exchanged addresses and promised to remain in touch.[6]

Christina labored on. With Andreas's help, she found a position
at the university's psychology department. The pay was only one
hundred dollars a month but it was a way to get out of the house
and avoid her unresolved marital and in-law issues.[7]

During this time Andreas devoted himself energetically to his academic advancement, which he now realized depended on publication
as much as teaching. In September 1949 he published his first article
in the *American Economic Review*, a good vehicle to attract the attention of his peers. Entitled "Market Structure and Monopoly Power,"
it identified the author as an associate (rather than assistant) professor

of economics, indicating rapid progress from only two years before when Harvard told him he would have to remain at the instructor level for at least three years.

The article analyzes basic characteristics of the market and elements of industrial capacity and behavior that promote or inhibit free competition. It then seeks to construct a mathematical coefficient that can be employed to determine when monopoly power is exercised and to what extent. In a footnote at the end of the article Papandreou comments: "It may not be amiss to indicate the manner in which the concepts developed in this paper may be put to use in interpreting antitrust legislation. The Sherman Act, for instance, takes on a much clearer meaning for the economist when couched in terms of the concepts presented in this paper, than it would otherwise possess."[8]

This may well be true for the economist. For the lay reader, the theoretical nature of Papandreou's model and the absence from it of such empirically generated variables as quality control and outlay for promotion of the product would seem to limit its practical utility. Nevertheless, the article generated interest among economists and, according to Nick Papandreou, became known as the "Papandreou coefficient."[9] Purely from the standpoint of assessing Andreas's personal priorities and outlook at this stage of his life it is interesting to note his desire to present theoretical concepts in a juridical framework attuned to the concerns of government in a capitalist society.

Papandreou continued looking for ways to reconcile theoretical economic concepts with real-life economic experience. In 1950 he delivered an address to the Midwest Economic Association that was published by the *Economic Journal* under the title "Economics and the Social Sciences." In this presentation Andreas defined what he termed a "back room–front room" approach to economics. The back room contained conceptual schemes that were "designed to impose restrictions on ... the operationally defined economic variables" to be found in the front room.[10] (One is permitted to wonder why experientially derived variables would not more logically impose restrictions on theoretical concepts than the reverse.) In his concluding paragraph Papandreou theorizes about the direction his fellow economists should be looking in the 1950s: "The maxim that the economist of our day should observe is open-mindedness towards the achievements of other social sciences. The future of economics as an empirical science may well depend on the degree to which our generation of economists are [*sic*] willing to live by it."[11] Here, too, Andreas seems to tiptoe around the relationship between economics and "other social sciences." Political science? He may have been thinking of the Roosevelt administration's enhanced power over private industry during World War II.

In the summer of 1950 George Papandreou made an official visit to Washington and Andreas and Christina traveled east to join him. Meeting her father-in-law for the first time, Christina was both flattered and nonplussed by his attentions. Like Andreas, she found him a man of great charm and even greater vanity, a tall, imposing figure with strong features, the nose of a Roman emperor and deep-set, penetrating eyes under a high forehead. Only his chin, she thought, betrayed a certain weakness.

An unabashed philistine, with little interest in the capital's cultural attractions, George Papandreou spent much of his visit alternately playing the stern father with Andreas and the ladies' man with Christina—another facet of the complex relations between father and son. He presented his daughter-in-law with gifts, clasped her around the shoulders, and stroked her wrists when they sat next to each other at dinner. At the same time Christina felt that his attitude toward her was quite patronizing. Her medical degree prompted only a question as to whether a healthy sex life contributed to good health in general. When she nodded, he smiled in satisfaction. He was fond of saying that before marriage a man was a woman's slave; after marriage, it was the other way around. There was no irony in his voice when he pronounced this homily. She concluded that he was less interested in consulting her than impressing her. As far as her role in marriage was concerned the elder Papandreou left no doubt what was expected of her. "A woman is not a woman until she gives birth," he reminded her pointedly.[12]

Greece was the only country that really interested George Papandreou, and its politics were his lifeblood. Why Andreas chose to remain in the United States perplexed him, and in front of Christina he tried to convince his son to return. "All Greece awaits you," he said. When Andreas replied that his future lay in the United States, his father bellowed, "What can a Papandreou become in the United States? A university professor. A nothing!" Christina chimed in to defend her husband, claiming that he had already become "one of the five most distinguished economists in the world." Her hyperbole got her nowhere. George Papandreou asked dismissively, "Really? Who are the other four?" and smiled triumphantly when Christina was unable to name them.

The distance between father and son notwithstanding, there were moments when Christina glimpsed another side to their relationship. One evening as she approached the two from a distance, she saw them standing in the hotel lobby, talking animatedly, laughing at some shared recollection, and taking such obvious pleasure in each other's company that she was momentarily overcome by a mixture of tenderness and envy. For her own father, she adds innocently, such intimate laughter could only indicate a guilty secret.[13] Given that Andreas was already involved with Margaret at the time, what an irony it would have been if in this case her father had been right—that the philandering father and son *were* sharing a guilty secret.

George Papandreou's entreaties did not end with his departure. He wrote, he telephoned, and he even enlisted the help of the then Greek prime minister Nicholas Plastiras, who was briefly in Chicago while Andreas was teaching for a semester at nearby Northwestern University. Their encounter is described by Andreas's close friend Adamantios Pepelasis, in a memoir devoted in large part to the ups and downs of his own relationship with him. Plastiras's effort to lure Andreas back to Greece was futile, and upon his return to Athens he reported to George Papandreou that not only was Andreas firm in his refusal but that "his feelings toward us are not particularly warm."[14]

George Papandreou soldiered on. Pepelasis was present during a later father-son conversation in Athens sometime in 1961, when

Andreas was doubting whether his decision to stay in Athens and start up an economic research center had any chance of success. "Think, Andreas," his father said, "if you die in America, how many people will come to your funeral? Then think how many will follow your casket in Athens if you stay."[15] Pepelasis does not comment on how the chairman of the economics department at Berkeley reacted to this lugubrious appeal, but he, too, would eventually break with his friend when Andreas became a disruptive member of the Center Union Party.

As an ambitious thirty-year-old in Minneapolis, however, Andreas was thinking less of his casket than of his colleagues in the economics department, three of whom received promotions after the 1948–49 academic year. Although they were older and had been on the faculty considerably longer than himself, Christina writes that Andreas was "frantic" about his failure to be included.[16] Once again he began casting his net, and when he secured a semester's visiting professorship at Northwestern University, he took his mother to look after him, not Christina. In her absence, Andreas and Margaret resumed their affair, in the course of which Margaret separated amicably from her husband and Andreas more bitterly from Christina. According to her, it was Sophia who broke the news of Andreas's decision to start divorce proceedings, and only afterward did he write Christina himself, asking her not to tell anyone, lest his position at the University of Minnesota be jeopardized. She granted this last selfish request, returned to the East Coast, and told him "to do whatever he wanted."[17]

Reunited after an emotionally fraught year, Andreas and Margaret went together to Reno, Nevada, the capital of quickie divorces, and became man and wife in a civil ceremony on August 30, 1951. (Although neither held any profound religious convictions, for social and political reasons they were remarried ten years later by a Greek Orthodox priest with their four children in attendance.)[18]

The couple immediately moved back to Minneapolis for the 1951 academic year and lost no time starting a family. Son George was born there in 1952 and daughter Sophia in 1954. Following Greek custom, the children were named for Andreas's parents, but by this time Andreas was so Americanized that little Sophia went by her middle name, Gail, and to his friends and colleagues Andreas was known as Andy. During his four subsequent years at the University of Minnesota, he became a passionate aficionado of American jazz and as active as Margaret in Minnesota's liberal politics. He chaired the local campaign committee for Adlai Stevenson in 1952, and with office mate Walter Heller (future chairman of President John F. Kennedy's Council of Economic Advisors) and his wife, the young Papandreous huddled together in front of a black-and-white television set to bemoan Stevenson's defeat to Dwight Eisenhower.

In every way Andreas's second marriage was the antithesis of his first. In Margaret he had found a romantic and true political soul mate, a confident, fun-loving woman who quickly gave him two children and the promise of more. His faintly accented English and remnants of Old World mannerisms made him popular with both students and colleagues. Now in his early thirties, he had everything he wanted—including his mother, who had returned to Greece while Andreas and Margaret were working out their complicated romance but rejoined the household when Margaret became pregnant with George. Whatever difficulties Margaret had to resolve with Sophia, she had two strikes in her favor: she made Andreas happy, and she made babies. Two more sons, Nicholas and Andreas, were born in 1956 and 1958, by which time the Papandreous had moved to Berkeley.

Andreas's years at the University of Minnesota were his most productive from the standpoint of publication. His articles, coauthored in most cases with other faculty members, showed a continued focus on the entrepreneur, the firm, and the behavior of the firm in the marketplace, the same preoccupations that had led his Harvard colleagues to believe that his approach to the subject was closer to the Business School than the Department of Economics. In 1952, for example, the University of Minnesota published a volume to which he contributed an article under the title "Some Basic Problems with the Theory of the Firm." In 1953 he published an article esoterically entitled "The Experimental Test of an Axiom in the Theory of Choice," indicating a return to the study of entrepreneurial decision-making that had been central to his doctoral dissertation. In 1954 he coauthored a paper entitled "Testing Assumptions Underlying Economic Predictions" that dealt with other variables of intrinsic concern to entrepreneurs. It was published in the University of Minnesota's *Business News Notes*.

That same year Papandreou also published his most substantial contribution to economic studies. Brought out by a major publisher of nonfiction, Prentice Hall, and coauthored with department colleague J. T. Wheeler, it is a 594-page doorstop entitled *Competition and Its Regulation*.[19] According to Nicholas Papandreou, this was the work of which his father remained the proudest. Today, more than half a century after its publication, one can understand why. *Competition and Its Regulation* is a thorough and dispassionate analysis of the problems inherent in the attempts of government to create and sustain through legislation what the authors call a "workably competitive economy." Acknowledging the practical difficulty of distinguishing between unacceptably "aggressive behavior" on the part of a firm and a desirable degree of "vigorous competitive behavior," Papandreou and Wheeler examine in detail legal actions initiated by the federal government under the Sherman and Clayton Acts and related antitrust legislation, to prevent or repair the damaging effects on competition of either vertical or horizontal monopolies. They go on to make specific proposals to improve existing legislation.[20] Portions of the book make interesting reading today, considering more recent examples like the U.S. government's failed suit against Microsoft Corporation for allegedly creating a virtual monopoly that blocked the entry of competing firms into the software marketplace. It is worth noting that in their examination of corporate behavior the authors of *Competition and Its Regulation* are not opposed to largeness per se. On the contrary, they recognize that greater size enables a firm to develop new technologies and innovations beyond the capacity of small business. They seek to inhibit corporate monopoly without stifling corporate growth.

It is impossible to attribute specific chapters to a specific coauthor. However, knowing Papandreou's path from law into economics we may assume that most of the case analysis is his work. In view of his earlier (and later) embrace of radical socialism I quote a paragraph at the beginning of the book in which the authors state one of the essential assumptions underlying the issue of government intervention in a private enterprise economy: "The strength of the faith in individualism and rationalism is such in our society that even the socialists, in attacking the laissez-faire and private enterprise economy, have attempted to construct a model which preserves them both. It is interesting to note, however, that the socialists have been unable to persuade our society that, *in fact*, a planned economy is consistent with individualism. So in our society the faith in individualism implies a faith in an unplanned and private enterprise economy."[21] Whether or not Papandreou composed these words himself, they certainly suggest how much he had come to identify himself with American values and economic priorities.

As an associate professor at the University of Minnesota Andreas was earning between seven and eight thousand dollars a year, a respectable income that allowed the Papandreous to take an ill-fated holiday in Greece in 1953. Along with Margaret, Adam Pepelasis witnessed Andreas's strange collapse and also believed that his physical paralysis was caused by traumatic memories of his arrest and beating by the Metaxas police in 1939.[22] And after seeing Andreas in the presence of his father, Margaret would become aware of the emotional memories he had suppressed while in the United States but which would resurface the more he felt the lure of a political career in Greece. Over the course of their thirty-year marriage she too came to recognize the duality of Andreas's character but, unlike Christina, was better equipped to hold that character—and her marriage—in balance in the maelstroms to come.

By the time *Competition and Its Regulation* was published in 1954, Papandreou's reputation among academic economists was so well established that other universities wanted to recruit him. With enthusiastic recommendation from Walter Heller, in 1955 the University of California at Berkeley offered Andreas a full professorship. The flagship campus was seeking to revitalize its economics department and repair a split on the faculty between modernists and traditionalists, which is to say between proponents of the "new" economics, based primarily on mathematically constructed models, and the old, relying on traditional methods of research and explication. The faculty's inability to agree on new appointments had left many vacancies unfilled. Papandreou's approach to economics would have placed him in the modernist camp, but his teaching years had demonstrated his ability to work well with economists of the older school. His affability, combined with his reputation as a relatively apolitical economist, convinced California's search committee that he was the man for the job.

Within two years he was department chair, assembling a faculty that many of his contemporaries considered the best in the United States. So successful was he in identifying and recruiting new talent, including from Harvard, that McGeorge Bundy, then Harvard's dean of the Faculty of Arts and Sciences, lamented to a colleague, "Every time the sun shines in Berkeley it's a dark day in Cambridge."[23] According to Professor Dale Jorgensen of Harvard (himself one of those bright young economists recruited by Papandreou), three of Andreas's picks went on to win the Nobel Prize in Economics and eight were elected to the National Academy of Science.[24] By any standard this is a remarkable record.

Moving into university administration inevitably meant less time for teaching, research, and publication. At California Papandreou collaborated with colleagues on several econometric studies, produced his monograph on *Stochastic Theory of Choice*, and in 1958 published his first individually written book, *Economics as a Science*, but his serious scholarship in economics was for the most part behind him.

One of his managerial projects was to acquire a digital computer for his department. These were the early days of computers, and the technology was cumbersome and expensive. Only the hard sciences departments had justified their need for a computer, and to do so for the economics department Andreas had to go before the university's Digital Computer Committee, headed by the imperious physicist Edward Teller, the "Father of the Hydrogen Bomb."

As Papandreou recounted the story to me, he was apprehensive at the prospect of being grilled by Teller ("When he looked at you, you could almost see the mushroom cloud"), and so he followed the advice of colleagues in the hard sciences, who had gone through the ordeal, to take along the best mathematician in his department for support. Andreas chose a twenty-something instructor who had impressed him by his extraordinary ability to play with mathematical abstractions. On the appointed day Teller, flanked by two colleagues, sat at a raised dais in front of a long blackboard and snapped at Andreas, "Who vill go to zee blackboard?" Andreas pointed to his colleague, and after some brusque questions to the instructor from Teller, for the next hour the only sound in the room was the squeak of chalk on the board. When it was filled with calculations, Teller dismissed the mathematician with a wave of the hand, turned to Andreas, and barked, "I take it vee are agreed zat zee economics department has tzustified its need for a deezital computer." The uncomprehending economics chairman had not uttered a word.

Although fully confident in his persona, Papandreou remained sensitive to newcomers' insecurities, especially if they were, like himself, foreign born. Harvard professor Henry Rosovsky once reminisced with me how he had arrived with a "refugee psychology" that Andreas had helped him overcome by introducing him to American mores. "Not always successfully," he chuckled. When Rosovsky and his wife were looking to buy a used car, Andreas insisted on accompanying them from one car lot to another, and when Rosovsky was tempted by a Ford, Andreas convinced him to buy an older Chrysler instead. "You're a gentleman," he said. "A Ford is not a gentleman's car." The Chrysler turned out to be a lemon, but Rosovsky never forgot how the thoroughly Americanized Andreas had reached out to a newly arrived immigrant.[25]

Following his second return from Athens to Berkeley in 1962, the University of California's visionary chancellor Clark Kerr shortlisted Papandreou for the chancellorship of the University of California at Santa Cruz, one of its new satellite campuses. Andreas had departed Athens in an angry mood ("Greece is no place for me," he had told Margaret) and the potential promotion reinforced his decision to leave. Yet no sooner was he back in Berkeley than he changed his mind, telling Margaret that even if offered the chancellorship he would refuse. Already regretting his decision to quit Athens, he fell into a deep mental depression compounded by headaches and stomach pains, which Margaret nursed him through until the cloud lifted and Andreas resigned from the University of California at the end of 1962.[26] As they toasted in the New Year Margaret knew that this was the turning point—that for her restless, mercurial husband his sabbatical in 1959 and second return to Greece in 1961 were just the beginning of his journey home.[27]

5

The Years of Our Greek Experience

IN 1959 THERE were no apartment buildings in Psychiko, no lack of parking space on the streets, and the commute to Syntagma (Constitution Square) in downtown Athens was an easy run down the main artery, Kifissia Boulevard. Except for kiosks, packed with newspapers and sundries, and the occasional cries of itinerant tinkers and green grocers hawking their wares, there was little commercial bustle to disturb Psychiko's countrified air. It was a purely residential suburb, built with old money and solid bourgeois taste. The stone and stucco houses were a mix of Balkan, neoclassical, and Bauhaus architecture, exuding respectability without ostentation. Even the several properties built by the royal family were relatively unpretentious, although long after they were sold, they were still known as "Prince or Princess So-and-So's house."

Off Kifissia Boulevard, the main entrance to Psychiko was its broadest and straightest street, Diamandidou. It rose gradually uphill and had two large rotaries (*plateias*) with narrow streets leading off them toward smaller *plateias* with more offshoots. It was easy to get lost in Psychiko, and the best way to get a sense of its meandering streets, tidy houses, and little domed churches set like puddings among pines and cypresses was atop a rock quarry bordering the next suburb, Philothei. From there one could also take in Mount Hymettos, the whale-backed mountain that separates Athens and its northern suburbs from the sea.

Toni and I lived just off Diamandidou at 24 Guizi Street, in what must have been Psychiko's smallest house, a whitewashed cube with a wall in front and a garden behind, scented by two fig trees and a shady grape arbor. Perhaps the first owners were newlyweds like us or an elderly retired couple with no need of extra bedrooms—except, of course, the prerequisite one in the basement for a live-in maid. Ours, whose hardscrabble journey from village peasant to urban domestic covered all the milestones of wartime Greece, rejoiced in the boiler's warmth and a bed of her own. She stuffed her wages under her mattress and every now and then exchanged the paper currency for a gold sovereign. With vivid memories of the inflation years, when shoppers lugged suitcases of drachmae to buy food for the day, Martha didn't trust any money she couldn't break a tooth on.

Nearby, at 58 Guizi Street, stood Andreas's childhood home. It was a spacious villa, somewhat modernized by a Danish living room set and a stereo console but otherwise much as it must have been when he lived there with his mother. Although Sophia was a household fixture, we came to know her mostly as a shy presence who tended to withdraw when the Papandreous had visitors.

We met Margaret and Andreas at a typically animated bilingual dinner party given by a Liberal Party deputy and his Greek American wife. Then the youngest member of Parliament, John Boutos would go on to serve in a variety of ministerial posts in several Greek governments, crossing and recrossing the indistinct lines that separated the parties of the center and the right. His wife, Mary, was heir to the Evga ice cream company, deservedly the most popular and well-marketed brand of frozen desserts in Greece. It was the first to play musical jingles on its bicycle carts, inspired by the Good Humor trucks her family had known in the United States. In the heat of a Greek summer, they were like the music of the spheres.

The Papandreous were a striking couple who made deceptively different first impressions. Margaret's slightly guarded manner seemed to imply that she suspended friendship until she could judge the stranger she was talking to. Her son Nick described her as "an impressive brunette born in a working-class suburb of Chicago whose father taught her to work hard, live clean, and not complain about the weather."[1]

Andreas, on the other hand, seemed completely unguarded. He had a warm smile and a manner which implied, or which people inferred, that you were exactly the person he had hoped to meet that evening and that your opinions were exactly those he wanted to hear. He too was tall, though not as tall as his famous father. Nor did he yet have George Papandreou's craggy features and overpowering vocal cords. At age forty, Andreas's hairline was beginning to recede, but his eyebrows were thick and black, highlighting deepset, intelligent eyes that seemed appraising without being critical, observant rather than wary. With his agreeable manner and ever-so-faintly accented English, he presented himself as no less and no more than what he was: a worldly economics professor, totally at ease in his surroundings.

Papandreou and I were seated next to each other, and when I explained who I was and how I had already met his father, Andreas was eager to hear my thoughts on the Greek political scene. He was a newcomer, he said, focused on the economy, and his first impression of Greek parliamentarians was how little interest they took in it. The state's coffers, he explained, were overly reliant on external sources of income, like emigrant remittances, shipping, and tourism, without thought to developing Greece's natural resources. Furthermore, the few raw materials that Greece did export were more profitable to importing countries than to Greece because that was where value was added. Greek hides sold to Italy were turned into Gucci shoes; Greek bauxite was processed into aluminum in France; Greek tobacco was blended into expensive cigarette brands in Egypt and the Levant.

Just as discouraging, he continued, was to see how Italy promoted its marble worldwide while Greece's even better-quality marble was used locally for pavement and dish-shattering kitchen sinks. Was it due to inefficiency, poor infrastructure, bad marketing, or a combination of all three? The same could be asked of Greek olive oil, succulent fruits, and dairy items like feta, the goat cheese that northern

Europeans made an inferior version of, under the same name. The best way to tackle the problem, Andreas believed, was to approach it "scientifically," without political preconceptions. For this opportunity he thanked Prime Minister Karamanlis, who struck Andreas as a forward thinker, a leader who seemed to put national interests above party ones. Washington and the American embassy thought the same. This was Karamanlis's second term in office; he had already been minister of labor and minister of public works and was greatly esteemed in official American circles for his efficient deployment of American aid in rebuilding Greece's infrastructure.

When the conversation shifted, as it always did, to the latest Cyprus crisis, Andreas had little to say. The island, with its majority Greek population, was still a British colony, and in 1959 Greece was involved in tortuous negotiations with the United Kingdom and Turkey over whether Cyprus should be independent or reunited with the motherland—the perennial goal of all Greek governments. Once again "*Enosis!*" (Union!) was the topic of the day in Parliament and on the streets. This goal, however, was severely stymied by the inconvenient fact that 18 percent of the island's population was Turkish, making *enosis* an unrealistic policy and independence the only logical solution—as it turned out to be in the London-Zurich accords of 1960. Throughout the heated discussion, however, Andreas pulled on his pipe and played the neutral observer. But then, I reminded myself, why shouldn't he? He wasn't Greek; he was American.

After discovering that we were near neighbors we began to see each other often. Toni introduced Margaret to the better stalls at the Friday open-air market, to the little old lady who mended nylon stockings, and to the butcher who kept scraps of meat for our dog. One morning Andreas knocked on our door with his own dog in tow and asked if we could keep it for the day—not because they were going away but because his father was coming over. "We haven't told him about the dog," Andreas said sheepishly. Like many Greeks, especially of his generation, George Papandreou considered dogs a filthy breed, totally unsuitable as household pets. We sympathized with Andreas's predicament and promised not to say a word. Still, it was an odd situation when a forty-year-old man had to conceal a fondness for dogs from his own father.

Over the hill in the adjoining suburb of Philothei was an outdoor restaurant that served the best souvlaki around. The four of us went there on occasion, and after licking our skewers clean and sopping up the salad's last drops of olive oil with chunks of country bread, we strolled next door to an open air cinema whose projector might, or might not, hold up for the duration of the film. Andreas's taste in movies was uncomplicated: nothing avant-garde or, as Ronald Reagan once said about historical costume clunkers, nothing "where the hero writes with a feather."

Andreas was partial to gangster films, the more shoot-ups the better. Somewhat incongruously, he was a crack shot and a fancier of firearms. I witnessed this one night when we slipped away early from a stag function, and Andreas suggested we stop at an amusement park. He headed straight for the shooting gallery and proceeded to knock out more ducks than there were Kewpie doll prizes. Years later Andreas told me about a grisly boyhood accident that had led to his skill as a marksman. He was sitting on a pier, watching some fishermen, when one of them swung back his line and lodged the fishhook in Andreas's left eye. The guilt-stricken fisherman managed to remove the hook by hand but his amateur efforts left Andreas with permanently impaired vision in the eye. To avoid risking further damage to his vision he stopped playing field sports at school and took up target shooting, for which only one good eye was needed.

The months passed, and the more I saw of Andreas, the more I sensed that I had become a sort of respite for him as he navigated his way through the Greek bureaucracy and around his father's demands. Sitting under our grape arbor, safely out of paternal earshot, he'd put his feet up on a chair and launch into sorry tales of the nepotism, indifference, and lazy work habits he had to put up with at government ministries. Three janitors to change a light bulb? Five clerks filling out a dozen forms to request a document, and two weeks to retrieve it? Well, he'd chuckle, it was one way to boost employment figures. "Why *anybody* would want to run this country . . ." he once began, and then thought better of the answer. His father was always the elephant in the grape arbor.

George Papandreou's ambitions for Andreas were likely magnified by his disappointment in his younger son, also named George, the offspring of his affair with Kyveli. Young George suffered from some sort of psycho/physiological disorder that in those days went unmentioned in public. We met him once or twice at Kastri, where he was trotted out briefly and then expected to disappear. Andreas would greet him kindly and exchange a few words before turning his attention to the other guests. Observing them together I sometimes wondered if despite their disparate lives they shared similar feelings about their father, a mixture of attraction and estrangement that may have contributed to Andreas's periodic illnesses and to the disoriented personality of his half brother.

Although George Papandreou had gained national recognition as minister of education in the 1930s (building hundreds of rural schools and importing great quantities of Swedish timber to do so), he never considered teaching a serious profession. To him, politics was a man's highest calling, and if Andreas had thought otherwise for twenty years, there were now signs that he was tempted to extend his stay in Greece. Karamanlis had met with Andreas to discuss how to best put his suggestions for economic reform into action. Andreas replied with a proposal to create an economic research institute, staffed by skilled technocrats capable of imposing long-range policies, both public and private, that would bring Greece's economy into the twentieth century. Andreas had already batted the idea around with economists in the United States, one of whom, Carl Kaysen, had come to Greece on a research study of his own. The two men became close friends and collaborators on what would become the Economic Research Center, or KOE. (When the Kennedy administration appointed Kaysen to the National Security Council, American investment in KOE looked even more promising.)

Andreas began to recruit the best and brightest among his contacts in academia and think tanks; for funding he turned to the Ford and Rockefeller Foundations, both known for their support of the New Frontier's policy to keep underdeveloped countries like Greece in the democratic camp by promoting robust economic modernization. The Economic Cooperation Administration (ECA), formerly the Marshall Plan, was also shifting aid from western to southern Europe and the newly independent African states. For its part, with behind the scenes maneuvering by George Papandreou, the Greek government arranged to put Andreas on its payroll by appointing him advisor to the Bank of Greece.

If Andreas was dipping his toe into Greek waters, he was doing it cautiously and with the mindset of an American Cold War liberal. In his pitch to the Ford and Rockefeller Foundations he spoke of "nation building" and "Western" reforms that would help prevent "the spread of communism." But once KOE's funding was secured and his position as director announced, Andreas began to waver. Anxious to keep his position (and salary) at the University of California, he pondered spending half his time in Berkeley and half at KOE. In the end he decided to go home first and think the matter over.

Despite the fact that Papandreou was the son of his archrival, Karamanlis had reasons of his own to support KOE and its new director. The prime minister was under pressure from his own party (and Washington) to do more—or at least appear to do more—about the country's flat economy and rising unemployment. Both were believed to have contributed to the communist-led United Democratic Left (EDA) taking second place in the 1958 elections, pushing the Liberal Party out of contention and reducing ERE's margin of victory. In any case, Andreas was an American, an economist with no experience in Greek politics.

At times Andreas felt the same way, one day on the phone with KOE recruits and the next day calling them back to say the project was hopeless. George Papandreou thought otherwise. This was his son's first step into public affairs in Greece, and he firmly believed it would lead him into politics. One evening, over the dinner table at Kastri, he spoke jubilantly about Andreas's future as leader of the

The Years of Our Greek Experience

Liberal Party. He looked to me to second the motion but my short response was that if his son did stay in Greece he should stick to his profession. The problem with Greece, I whispered to Andreas, was that it had too many politicians and too few economists. He laughed heartily, and when his father asked what was so funny, he said we were just sharing an untranslatable American joke.

Dinners at Kastri usually began late, after Parliament's evening session, and sometimes ended in the wee hours with a tour of the rose garden. The elder Papandreou loved roses, and he loved playing the courtly host. Well into his seventies, his fondness for pretty women was undiminished, and if one took his fancy, he would present her with a single rose that he picked every day and displayed in a bud vase on a side table. Sometimes, after dinner, he'd put a dance record on a Victrola—a waltz, a fox trot, or a tango—and then swoop up his partner of choice for a few whirls. Since Toni was a willowy blonde and an accomplished dancer, she tangoed many nights away and took home many roses.

Our Greek vocabulary grew exponentially from the many political and idiomatic expressions the Papandreou circle used among themselves. That Toni and I were so casually included was due, I believe, as much to calculation as friendship, as well as company for Margaret, who was just beginning to learn Greek. That first year her natural reserve and genuine puzzlement when Greeks talked to each other—which was everybody at once—made me wonder at times if she would ever feel comfortable in George Papandreou's world. She was unfailingly courteous toward him, tactful in her remarks, but not self-effacing, and much less submissive, unlike the diffident behavior he expected of a proper Greek wife.

The more we came to know her, the more we admired her calm but independent character. What we had taken for aloofness was really thoughtfulness; and if she remained, to a degree, on guard, it was less against others than to protect herself against certain changes in her relationship with Andreas that were bound to arise after their move to Athens. He was more social, more open in conversation, but his convictions and loyalties were shallower than hers. Over the course of their marriage Margaret would prove the stronger of the two, adjusting to his many moods as he weighed his future and casting her lot with him when he chose to return permanently to Greece.

But such a future was still conjecture when Andreas finished his sabbatical and the family returned to Berkeley in August 1960. In company with Andreas's father and a parade of well-wishers bearing outsized floral arrangements and overflowing baskets of food, we trooped up the gangway of the *Queen Frederika* to see them off. For Toni and me it was a temporary adieu; in October we would be taking home leave in California and planned a reunion with the Papandreous in Berkeley and Carmel, my boyhood home. For George Papandreou it was a bitter farewell. Even in the crowded cabin he tried to convince Andreas that his place was in Greece but received only a promise to visit the following summer. When we disembarked his father was in tears, waving his handkerchief until the ship was out of sight.

In Margaret's later account to me, the farewell proved equally wrenching for Andreas, but for more complicated reasons.[2] Much as he and Margaret had talked about the pros and cons of staying in Greece or going "home," no sooner had the *Queen Frederika* docked at its first port of call in Naples than Andreas announced that he had changed his mind and was now set on returning to Athens in January. He dashed down the gangway, calling over his shoulder that he had to telephone his father to give him the news.

Margaret was upset but not totally surprised. Andreas had worked frantically to set up the fledgling KOE and she innocently assumed that his desire to push the project to completion was the cause of his about-face. Only after their return did she realize that Andreas was infatuated with a young Greek woman who worked at the American aid mission.[3] As was often the case with Andreas, his professed motivations masked or became the rationale for his real ones.

In the two months between the Papandreous' departure and our own, we had two awkward encounters with George Papandreou. One Sunday, when I was the embassy's weekend duty officer, he showed up unannounced at our house. After Toni explained my absence,

The Years of Our Greek Experience

he lingered a while, as if weighing his options, and then suddenly swooped her up in a passionate embrace. Between his advanced years and Toni's youthful agility it was neither a conquest nor a contest. If anything, she said afterward, he was the embarrassed party, an aging Romeo who had foolishly believed she would be flattered by his attentions, while she found the incident totally ludicrous. Once rebuffed, however, he was the perfect gentleman with her thereafter.

But his belief that we could be helpful in his ambitions for his son was even more foolish. On another occasion he came to the house by prearrangement, this time to discuss the serious business of Andreas's future. He had been thinking about Margaret's place in it and had reached the conclusion that *she* was the major obstacle keeping Andreas from taking up a political career in Greece. Of course he couldn't, so long as he was married to an American, perpetually pulling him back to the United States. "Politics is in my son's blood," he rose to proclaim, as if addressing the crowds from a balcony, "it is his destiny!" Alas, he continued, as we listened in horrified silence, the subject of divorce was too delicate for him to raise, and therefore he wished us to do so in his stead. *Our* motives would not be misunderstood; Margaret would *realize* what was best for Andreas—for Greece!—and would step aside graciously.

I groped for a firm but tactful approach to dissuade the elder Papandreou of his outrageous, indeed perverse idea. We Americans were sentimental about marriage, I explained, and we frowned upon husbands who dispatched their wives for career purposes, however noble the cause. But should Andreas be considering a permanent return to Greece—his insistence to the contrary—he would need Margaret more than ever by his side. After all, she was the anchor of the household, tending to four young children, not to forget Andreas's mother, while he was free to follow his bent without domestic encumbrances. Whatever their personal relationship, any decision about their future together was an intensely private matter in which outsiders had no right to interfere. That was the way things worked in America, I finished emphatically. George Papandreou's face sagged in disappointment, but he did not pursue the subject further and took his leave quickly, embarrassed that he had overstepped the line.

When the younger Papandreous returned in January, Margaret began to suspect that Andreas's urgent telephone call to Athens from Naples was probably not to his father. He was spending more and more time with the young woman who had been helping him with facts and figures about our aid program. She came from a prominent conservative family; her uncle was a member of Parliament and a staunch supporter of Karamanlis, the army, and its commander in chief, the king. Before long, Andreas's involvement with her reached his father's ears, and according to Margaret, he counseled his son only to be more discreet and not make any rash promises. "Don't make the same mistake I made," he warned him, referring to his own well-publicized affair with Kyveli. Although they married, the union was tumultuous, and ended in divorce.[4]

Considering how much George Papandreou disapproved of his son's American marriage, one might suppose he would smile favorably on the prospects of a Greek one. But in Greece's contentious, clannish political world, linking the proudly republican Papandreou family to an avowedly royalist one was as frowned upon as marrying into a different social class in Great Britain or a different race in the United States. The trysting couple may have felt the same way, or Andreas may have still felt American enough to feel guilty about the affair, which ended without public awareness. (After his third marriage, Margaret told me that Andreas was never a casual philanderer, but rather a "serial monogamist.")

Toni and I arrived in California shortly after John F. Kennedy's victory in the November 1960 presidential election. After showing us around Berkeley the Papandreous spent a weekend with us in a cottage we had rented down the coast in Carmel. We spent most of it discussing the incoming Kennedy administration and what it might portend for Greek-American relations.

Andreas was pleased to see the new president drawing on academic talent, especially among his old colleagues, and had already been in touch with them by letter and phone. They included John

Kenneth Galbraith and Carl Kaysen from Harvard and Walter Heller from the University of Minnesota. Caught up in the excitement of the day, we anticipated a Kennedy team that would bring renewed vigor to Washington and, given Andreas's contacts there, a sharper interest in his role at KOE, to which he was now enthusiastically planning to return, apparently with the University of California's blessing.

Meanwhile, Athens's thirteen daily newspapers ran as much, if not more, coverage of the new American administration than at home, most of them assuming with customary parochialism that the New Frontier's first order of business would be to choose which party to back in the next Greek elections. Would the youthful new president instinctively support the Liberals in their struggle to gain power, or was Karamanlis still the man of the hour? They searched for clues: Was it true that someone with a Greek name was on the White House staff? That Jacqueline Kennedy was an ardent philhellene, redecorating the White House in neoclassical style? She wasn't, but she did fill the pages of the fashion magazines, and 1961 became the year that Athenian ladies discarded their floral-print dresses for solid-colored shantung suits topped with pearl necklaces and pillbox hats.

Politically, the year in Greece was a problematic one. The American embassy and the Karamanlis administration were still assessing the fallout of EDA's second-place finish in the previous elections and the danger of its permanently displacing a more palatable centrist opposition. With the next election constitutionally required by the spring of 1962, a new strategy arose: to separate the patriotic sheep from the subversive goats by uniting the center parties and changing the distribution of parliamentary seats. Manipulating the methods of how seats were apportioned was a regular practice of Greek governments whatever their coloration, and the apportionment that had backfired in 1958 was a system called Reinforced Proportional Representation. The consensus now between the embassy and the ERE government was to replace it with a system of "Related Parties," designed to shrink EDA's representation in Parliament.

Under the Related Parties system there would still be two distributions of parliamentary seats: the first made to all parties in proportion to the votes they received in each electoral district, and the second according to their national percentage. Under the new law, however, only the two top parties would be eligible to enter the second distribution; all the others would have to declare their affiliation with one or the other, creating two groups of "related" parties. Since the two most likely winners would be ERE and EDA, it was assumed that the Liberal Party and an assortment of smaller centrist parties would choose to affiliate with the rightist ERE rather than the extremist left, making a comfortable majority to counter whatever number of seats EDA had won.

The Related Parties system, or *apparentement*, was French in inspiration and practice, thereby enhancing its democratic credentials and, it was hoped, its appeal to the leaders of the center parties whose cooperation was essential if the system was to work. Both the Greek government and the embassy were optimistic that George Papandreou, the driving force behind unifying the center parties and an unwavering anti-communist, would agree to the plan.

As for the palace, King Paul and Queen Frederika approved heartily, although their briefing came not from Karamanlis but from our embassy's CIA station chief. The Central Intelligence Agency's special relationship with the monarchy—and with the army—dated back to the onset of the Civil War when Great Britain and the United States saw the two institutions as bulwarks against communism and symbols of national unity. The CIA station chief was particularly close to Queen Frederika, who tended to call the shots and believed the CIA "got things done" more quickly and efficiently than the State Department. While our ambassadors had deep misgivings about these arrangements, Frederika's wishes were hard to disregard and, in any case, this anomalous channel of communication enabled the palace to maintain the convenient fiction that it was above meddling in the country's politics. The wife of the station chief was also included in the special relationship, often escorting the queen and her two daughters, Princesses Sophia and Irene, to our Military Post Exchange in downtown Athens, where they carted out baskets of luxury items unavailable on the Greek market. Such gestures did little to enhance the monarchy's reputation, or the CIA's.

At the queen's suggestion, the station chief had been supplying books on political theory to Crown Prince Constantine, a young man more interested in sports cars than the workings of democracy. Frederika was a Hohenzollern and her grandfather was Kaiser Wilhelm II, which may explain why she entrusted her son's political education to an intelligence agency.

In 1961 Constantine was turning twenty-one. Eager to display his authority as regent while his parents were on an official trip abroad, he brushed up on the merits of the Related Parties system and was as surprised as its crafters when George Papandreou flatly rejected the plan. His strenuous objections were based on the grounds that the Related Parties proposal would force all centrist voters, indeed all voters who were not hard communists, into propping up permanently conservative rule. Reducing the multiparty political system to two extreme choices would prevent a centrist/left coalition from ever coming to power unless it broke ranks with the right and joined forces with EDA. Given George Papandreou's burning ambition to head the said coalition he could scarcely agree to serve under Karamanlis.

The upshot was that Andreas was recruited to bring his father on board. It would be his first serious brush with what was openly known as "the American Factor" and the way it operated behind the scenes. Until then his relationship with the American embassy had been cordial and useful to both. He was a breath of fresh air, a pragmatic American eager to introduce modern Western reforms to Greece at a time when the United States was growing weary of keeping reasonably democratic Greek governments afloat. More than a few cablegrams to and from Washington were filled with longing for the Greeks to step up to the plate and manage their own affairs.

But the CIA station managed its own affairs badly by deciding to pair Andreas with the crown prince on a late-night mission to

Kastri, to persuade George Papandreou to change his mind. Both Margaret and Andreas describe the hasty visit in their books in the high-minded tone of Queen Victoria's "We are *not* amused." Margaret relates how they were about to sit down for dinner with friends when Andreas received a mysterious telephone call and left without explanation. Andreas continues the tale, about how he was summoned to the palace, where he waited over an hour for Constantine to appear, after which they jumped into the prince's sports car and tore off to Kastri.[5] By no means amused himself, George Papandreou held forth on the meaning of democracy and how the Related Parties plan would utterly destroy its bedrock principles. Constantine replied that the communist menace called for Papandreou to put national interest ahead of personal ambition and not waste time on speeches. Andreas was taken aback by the twenty-year-old's cavalier treatment of his father, who curtly ended the meeting. Apparently, Constantine accepted his failed mission with good humor and spent much of the wild drive back with his eyes off the road, showing off the incredible speed of his new Alfa Romeo.

According to Andreas, the arm twisting did not end there. Shortly after the midnight ride, he was approached by the CIA station chief, Laughlin Campbell, requesting another meeting with George Papandreou, this time with Andreas and himself. When Andreas tried to convince him that his father was unalterably opposed to the Related Parties system, he writes that Campbell became "angry and threatening." One need not accept Andreas's version of the encounter (Campbell was a man as little disposed to unpleasant confrontations as Andreas) to understand his dismay at having been roped into pressuring his own father on behalf of powerful outside forces. Now involved in the kind of Byzantine games he once hoped to avoid, he felt increasing loyalty to his father and admired his stubborn opposition. (By astutely holding his ground, George Papandreou hastened the Related Parties system's scarcely noticed demise and lived to fight another day.)

My own skepticism about the Related Parties plan was based on practical as much as ethical considerations. I doubted that the cen-

The Years of Our Greek Experience

ter parties, with their long republican tradition, would be willing to bury the past and align themselves, even for tactical purposes, with the Royalists and their right-wing allies. I also considered it unwise to pin the American flag on a project that had little chance of success and whose future consequences for Greek politics we had not adequately considered.

That said, the ongoing problem of how to forge a united non-communist opposition to conservative regimes remained, and while George Papandreou was making headway in that effort, his potential republican partners were an unpromising lot. Eleftherios Venizelos's republican legacy had passed to his son, Sophocles, a small, mustachioed man with a piping voice whose political skills were negligible and who, in any case, had become a royalist in everything but name. Despite its label, the Progressive Party led by Spyros Markezinis, a former minister credited with reining in Greece's runaway inflation after the civil war, was politically situated to the right of ERE. Prospects were further clouded by the recent entry into the political arena of General George Grivas. Grivas, who bore an unsettling resemblance to Groucho Marx, was even to the right of Markezinis, but he was something of a national hero because of the guerilla raids he had carried out against the British from secret bases in the Troodos Mountains of central Cyprus. His political appeal had yet to be tested, but there were many who still admired his sneak attacks on the British and anyone else who got in his way. George Papandreou had no respect for the rogue general. Asked by a journalist whether he thought Grivas would succeed in politics, Papandreou said scornfully, "How? He is famous only for hiding." This turned out to be a prescient observation and in due course Grivas faded from the scene. In 1961, however, his presence in the opposition added to the general uncertainty.

June, July, and August passed without visible progress for a unified coalition. What finally galvanized the disparate leaders into action was a surprise move by Karamanlis. Probably sensing that time would not always be on his side, in September 1961, scarcely after the Greeks had awoken from their August siestas, he called for early elections in October. The usual Reinforced Proportional Representation system would again be used, leaving the so-called coalition partners only six weeks to avoid the fate they had suffered in 1958. Whatever the bickering behind the scenes, they rallied at last under George Papandreou's leadership, and the newly proclaimed Center Union Party included all of the most prominent opposition figures except General Grivas and the leaders of EDA.

Time was short for the coalition to organize, articulate a message, and mount a campaign; but George Papandreou took heart from the large and enthusiastic crowds at his cross-country rallies, as did Andreas and Margaret, who were now accompanying him on the trail. There was no question that to many voters ERE had ruled long enough and that a change of government was due. Despite his officially neutral position at KOE, Andreas was soon totally absorbed in the contest and the possibility of his father winning it.

On the eve of the election, Toni and I squeezed into an overflowing throng at Syntagma Square to hear George Papandreou speak at his final rally. Following every party's practice of boosting attendance for the grand climax, the Center Union had bused thousands of followers in from the provinces, whose numbers, of course, would be inflated or deflated the next day by the partisan press. That night the scene was deafening, if not downright dangerous, as zealous supporters chanted slogans through amplified speakers and set off fireworks in the midst of the crowd. Music blared, sirens wailed, people fainted, and all around the square banners and outsized portraits of Papandreou flapped in the autumn wind. When one of his likenesses blew off its moorings, thousands of hands passed it to safety over their heads, as if rescuing a sailor from the waves.

When the Old Man, as he was affectionately called, appeared in person on a hotel balcony overlooking the square, he had to wait a good ten minutes for the brouhaha to subside. Then he began with his famous evocation of Pericles, "*Politai ton Athinon . . .*" and the citizens of Athens erupted again before finally settling on rhythmic chants between the great orator's sentences. I have no memory of Papandreou's speech, not that it mattered. This was a rally

The Years of Our Greek Experience

not to listen to but to be aroused by—to experience politics as theater, politics as a kind of catharsis.

We had been invited to a post-rally supper in Kastri. George Papandreou was in a buoyant mood. Surrounded by his *parea*, he basked in compliments on the enthusiasm and size of the crowd. The gaiety continued until dessert, when Papandreou halted the conversation and asked each of us at the table to predict the election's outcome. With a wicked glance, Toni passed the buck to me, the only other outsider. I had always been scrupulously neutral in my conversations with Papandreou about the Center Union's chances, and so I said only that the race between ERE and the Center Union was too close to call but that EDA would assuredly come in behind both.

In Greece, once an election is called for, the party in power is replaced by a service government to ensure neutrality throughout the campaign and to certify the results from the polling stations. During his whirlwind six weeks crisscrossing the country George Papandreou never expressed the slightest concern about the service government's impartiality or the possibility of irregularities at the polls. Indeed, he was supremely confident that he was on the threshold of the most important victory of his career, never more than at his election eve party, from which we staggered home just as the polls opened.

That confidence vanished when the returns came in. ERE won 51 percent of the popular vote and 176 seats in the 300-seat Parliament; the Center Union, 34 percent and 100 seats; and EDA, 15 percent and 14 seats. The results were gratifying to the Greek establishment and to the American embassy. Even without the Related Parties system the Center Union had vaulted into second place over EDA and become the recognized standard bearer of the democratic opposition. With the electoral pie satisfactorily divided, the powers that be breathed a sigh of relief. Certainly they expected George Papandreou to conclude that he had done rather well, given the rushed circumstances and open rivalry displayed by his coalition partners during the campaign.

But within a week Papandreou mounted the podium to accuse the service government, and by implication ERE, of stealing the election through "Fraud and Violence" (*Via kai Nothia*) and depriving him of legitimate victory. He vowed that his party would abstain or resign from Parliament unless new elections were called.

Via kai Nothia, Papandreou claimed, had deliberately kept opposition voters from the polls by drawing on anti-communist irregulars, the police, and the rural gendarmerie to scare them off or coerce them into choosing ERE ballots as they entered the polling station, where ballots were stacked openly on a table. In urban centers, and particularly in Athens, he charged massive malfeasance in voter registration and electoral tallies. And lastly, he asserted that the military vote had been grossly manipulated, producing over a 70 percent majority for ERE, a ridiculously implausible figure given the social diversity of the enlisted ranks.

Within the Center Union noisy disagreements erupted over how far the party's protests should go. Papandreou initially instructed his deputies to bring the issue to a head by refusing to take the oath of office, a tactic that could succeed only if all, or at least a great majority of them, refused en masse. They didn't, and within days Markezinis withdrew from the coalition, taking his bloc of Progressive Party deputies with him. Several independents followed, and among the remaining deputies there was little enthusiasm to give up their parliamentary privileges for a principled stand. In the end Papandreou had to settle for symbolic resistance: Center Union deputies would boycott the king's speech at the opening of Parliament on December 4; by December 9, they agreed to take the oath of office "under protest." EDA joined them, leading many to fear that their combined numbers might turn into populist uprisings, but EDA deputies proved to be as zealously protective of their parliamentary seats as the others.

In her book, Margaret states that she and Andreas remained outraged by the election results and that Andreas had urged his father to stand firm in his refusal to accept them. When George Papandreou retreated, Margaret recalls Andreas's disappointment in his father's "lack of vision."[6] It would be more accurate to say, "lack of a unified party." Andreas chose not to see it that way. He writes that he was proud of his father's efforts to keep the "Fraud and Violence" campaign alive, and when it began to falter, he describes his own efforts to sound alarm bells in Washington. He now refers to himself as his father's advisor, indicating that he was abandoning all pretense to neutrality and throwing his support to the Center Union.

Over the next months, Andreas and I had emotional discussions about the election results. I disagreed with him over the extent to which force and fraud had determined the Center Union's defeat but believed that with more coherence the party was bound to win the next time around. To ease his letdown I encouraged Andreas, should he continue to "advise" his father, to press the courts to investigate irregularities and punish those responsible. His replies varied: one day he railed against ERE, another against the Center Union for its irresolution. When he muttered that the Center Union needed fresh blood, I didn't ask whom he was thinking of.

On a trip to Thessaloniki he was clearly in a grievance mood, as one of our officers at the American Consulate General recounted for the State Department's Oral History archives:

> We discussed economics for twenty to thirty minutes before dinner. . . . At the dinner table, Andreas started to talk about the elections. Although he had been brought back to Greece by Karamanlis to set up an economic research center . . . he quickly became absorbed in Greek politics and was obviously a complete political animal. . . . It was clear that his heart was in politics and not in economics. He discoursed for four or five hours until midnight, just talking about the violence, the fraud that had been perpetrated. It was fascinating. I thought that this man was incredibly powerful and passionate but also a fanatic or zealot.[7]

The officer adds that "[Andreas] kind of muffled his attacks on the U.S. . . . it may have been that he hadn't reached the point to make an outright attack [on it]."

The irony of the embassy's reluctance to accept George Papandreou's accusations stemmed not only from his well-earned reputation for hyperbole but also from our decision *not* to send observers to polling stations on election day, precisely to avoid any charges of interference. We were left to investigate the contested figures after the fact; subsequently, in an evaluation that I drafted for the State Department, we acknowledged obvious manipulation of the military vote and examples of intimidation at certain polling stations but not widespread fraud in Athens. The dispatch went on to say:

> The Center Union, under the purple banner of Papandreou's oratory, has ridden off in all directions and in so doing has created much confusion about the real issues raised by the attack on the election results. These issues do not, as the Center Union would have us believe, pose the question, "who should govern Greece?" They do, however, raise important questions about the *way* Greece should be governed. . . . No serious observer of the Greek political scene believes that Papandreou and his ill-assorted coalition command as much popular confidence as Karamanlis. Many people do believe, however, that the Palace, the Army leadership and the internal security forces intervene too much in the political life of Greece and that the sluggishness of government administration, its apparent unresponsiveness to individual needs, has created a potentially dangerous gap between the governing class and the governed. . . . Greece, it is often said, is in mid-passage, but the phrase is usually used to describe a stage in the country's economic development. It is less widely understood that Greece is also in mid-passage socially and politically.

In retrospect, I believe that the embassy was too cavalier both in its dismissal of the most serious charges leveled by George Papandreou and in belittling his popular appeal. Only two years later he did become prime minister. We should also have questioned the fact that Karamanlis, whose vote percentage had dropped to 41 percent in 1958, rose to 51 percent in 1961, an unlikely turnabout for a party showing signs of decline. Furthermore, since a minor amount of coercion at the polls was accepted as common practice in Greece, we underestimated the lengths to which rightist apparatchiks would go to avoid repeating EDA's strong showing in 1958. All told, however, we were satisfied by Papandreou's hundred parliamentary seats and the prospect of Greek politics evolving into two major parties, free of communist influence and strong enough for one to replace the other without polarizing effects.

For the nonce there was Constantine Karamanlis, still respected for his political acumen. He was well practiced at knowing when or whether to distance himself from the palace, elements of the extreme right, and the Americans. He understood that twentieth-century Cold War politics were always a factor in Greek politics and was unsentimental in his methods to keep both in balance and himself in power.

In this respect George Papandreou looked old-fashioned by comparison. He was an emotional man, an eloquent spokesman for liberal causes, but in many ways he was a nineteenth-century figure, a Shakespearean actor who thrilled audiences with his rhetoric at the expense of the play. Famous for his role as the perennial leader of the opposition, he didn't need to turn words into action, only into protests against others' actions, real or perceived. By 1962 his cries for an "unyielding struggle" (*anenthotos agon*) against fraud and violence were wearing thin. Far from our expectations that Greece was entering a period of stability, it now seemed that George Papandreou was only reviving the kind of bitter partisanship that had plagued Greek politics so often before.

Enter the American ambassador to Greece. Ellis Briggs was a flinty old-school diplomat on his eighth assignment as chief of mission, many of them in longstanding dictatorships that had spared him the messy business of democratic elections. He regarded Greek politics as musical chairs with too many chairs and wanted little contact with any party other than ERE. In this frame of mind he issued a public statement congratulating Karamanlis on his victory, which, in his opinion, was demonstrable proof of "Greeks' and Americans' shared belief in personal freedom and the dignity of the individual."

This provoked howls in Parliament and the press, and when Ambassador Briggs departed Greece a few months later, the entire opposition boycotted his farewell reception.

In a way, so did Andreas. He had flown to the United States on a dual mission. One was to the Ford and Rockefeller Foundations to explain the changed situation in Greece after the fraudulent election and to tell them that, given his personal relationship and loyalty to his father's cause, he had no choice but to resign as KOE director. They urged him to stay on, but Andreas persisted and then, since he could no longer justify his position as advisor to the Bank of Greece, asked the Rockefeller Foundation to pay his salary through his remaining six months. After the foundation granted his request, he went to Washington to press home with his friends in the Kennedy administration certain facts of CIA skullduggery that he had personally experienced in Athens. He met with Carl Kaysen at the NSC and several high-ranking State Department officials whose bailiwicks included Greece. In *Democracy at Gunpoint* he notes with some satisfaction that he succeeded at getting the Athens CIA station chief expelled, although there is no evidence in cables from the State Department that the subject was ever raised there. Kaysen, whom I interviewed before his death, had no recollection of it.[8] Whether he made his case or not, Andreas remained an enthusiastic New Frontiersman, as did Margaret, and their campaign to drum up American support for a populist crusade in Greece fills many pages in their books. Andreas was even drawn to Arthur Schlesinger's stillborn project for the Kennedy administration to finance a worldwide "democratic movement," whether openly or covertly, and he may have begun to see himself as an agent for the cause. Certainly, he would have to be a secret agent if he were to continue directing KOE with the blessings of the conservative regime he wished to oust.

Throughout 1962 Andreas was increasingly tempted to stay in Greece, but he needed to have it both ways, or rather three ways: approval from the University of California to continue his leave of absence, an independent salary, and freedom to ally himself with the martyred Center Union. Not surprisingly, the university refused

The Years of Our Greek Experience

to grant him a third leave of absence and the Rockefeller Foundation made no promises to support him if he also engaged in partisan politics. Andreas then pursued a convoluted scheme to turn KOE into an independent international institute with no ties to any government. When that failed, he returned a second time to Berkeley to sort things out, financially and emotionally.

The months before his departure were not easy for Andreas, yet he put on a good face in public, continuing his contacts with the embassy, including the new ambassador, Henry Labouisse, a liberal who had agreeable relations with both Karamanlis and George Papandreou. Andreas also welcomed American visitors to KOE and made extra time to brief President Kennedy's youngest brother, Edward Kennedy, who was about to make his first run for the U.S. Senate. I left the briefing impressed as always by Andreas's presentation of KOE's mission to modernize the Greek economy. When the session ended Kennedy and Andreas relaxed over a bottle of scotch and engaged in banter about Richard Nixon's sallow complexion and five o'clock shadow that had cost him the first debate with the tanned, more youthful looking Jack Kennedy. The same could be said about the respective appearances of Teddy Kennedy and Andreas, the latter looking gaunt and exhausted from a recurring throat ailment and stomach pains that undoubtedly sprang from inner turmoil.

Margaret confirms that throughout 1962 Andreas was "leading a schizoid life . . . [seeing] events one day through the eyes of a Greek, the next through the eyes of an American."[9] Back in Berkeley he fell seriously ill with intestinal ailments that no doctors could diagnose. Margaret despaired for his recovery until Andreas finally healed himself and made up his mind: He was Greek. He was his father's heir. Politics was his destiny.

Still in Athens, Toni and I were under the impression that the Papandreous had gone home for good. They had talked wistfully of how restful it would be to look at San Francisco Bay instead of demonstrators at Syntagma Square. "Greece is no place for me," Andreas had confided to me as well as to Margaret; as if to confirm the fact, he gave us a parting gift, an inscribed copy of Theodore H. White's *The Making of the President, 1960*. On the flyleaf he had written: "To Monty and Toni, who have shared with us the years of our 'Greek experience.'"

After five years, our Greek experience was ending too. In January 1963 Toni and I were again on home leave in Carmel, relaxing with my mother and brushing up on our French before heading off to our next assignment to Léopoldville (now Kinshasa). Once again the Papandreous came to visit. The Congo was headline news, but Andreas was impatient to talk about Greece and his thoughts about going back. I wasn't sure what he meant. "To KOE?" I asked. He smiled enigmatically and said, "Well in *some* capacity. What do you think I should do?"

I launched into the pros and cons, mostly cons in my view, and for the rest of the evening we might have been back under the grape arbor, rehashing the problems he would be facing again, not least of them his father. Andreas nodded. "That's an excellent point," he interjected between my comments, but occasionally adding, "Patera is getting old. . . . Things are changing. . . . My job isn't done."

It took my mother, who knew absolutely nothing about Andreas, to see the obvious. "Well!" she exclaimed, after they had gone, "No doubt about it, he's a very smart man and a real charmer. But all that talk about Ko-Ay, or whatever you call that economic center, is a waste of time. He's a politician, and just like all politicians he smiles and sweet talks and agrees with everything you say. Then he goes off and does exactly what was in his mind the whole time."

Always listen to your mother.

6

Crises Everywhere

"LET THE WORD go forth that the torch has been passed to a new generation of Americans," President Kennedy proclaimed in his inaugural speech, "that we shall pay any price, bear any burden, meet any hardship . . . to assure the success of liberty . . . and the free world." We stood poised.

My assignment to Léopoldville in early 1963 as head of the Political Section was the most challenging one I had encountered to date. The crises that the newly independent Congo fell into after the Belgians' hasty exit were unrelenting: the assassination of the country's first prime minister, rebellions in the eastern provinces, and an inexperienced, incompetent government in the capital—all leading to a breakdown of civil order. In this fraught environment, the news of President Kennedy's assassination was a stunning shock. Toni and I were at a casual gathering of colleagues when someone rushed in, crying "The President has been shot . . . in Texas!" Automatically assuming that he meant the Congolese president, Toni blurted out, "In Texas? What on earth was Kassavubu doing in *Texas*?"

Around the world, not least in Léopoldville, mourners stood in line for hours outside our embassy to sign the condolence books and packed Léopoldville's cathedral to hear a stream of eulogies. In the middle of them, a colleague and I had to slip out when our walkie-talkies began to crackle with news of a rebel attack on an American missionary outpost, in which our consular officer and several missionaries were taken hostage. So ended that dreadful weekend.

Even on less somber occasions, the pace was frenetic. At the end of the week embassy staffers said to each other, "Thank God it's Friday. Only two more working days 'til Monday." For two and a half years the Congo was the center of our universe, and what news we got from elsewhere came from the BBC, which we picked up on a scratchy shortwave radio when it was not jammed by the Soviets.

I was generally aware that in June 1963 Karamanlis abruptly resigned his premiership over a dispute with the royal family and went into voluntary exile until new elections were called. I was less aware of Andreas's role in the ensuing crises over how the elections should be held but learned afterward from my successor in Athens that he had actively lobbied the American embassy and Washington to prevent another "Fraud and Violence" outcome. In November, George Papandreou achieved his goal, winning 42 percent of the electoral vote to Karamanlis's 39 percent and 138 Center Union parliamentary seats to ERE's 132. This was less than an outright majority, however, and to build on his momentum (and avoid having to form a coalition with EDA) Papandreou waited the constitutionally required forty-five days and then called for new elections in February 1964. These the Center Union won by a smashing 53 percent over ERE's 35 percent vote total and a comfortable majority of 171 seats in Parliament.

Andreas had never been confident that the Center Union would win the 1963 election, and despite heavy pressure from his father he declined to become a candidate himself. He did promise, however, that whenever the next election came around, he would run for his father's seat in Achaea. Undoubtedly unprepared for only a three-month interval, he honored his pledge nonetheless and resigned for good from KOE. The final leap came when he turned in his American passport and then called on Ambassador Labouisse to explain his decision. Labouisse wished him well in his run for a parliamentary seat, and when he won, I still believed that Andreas, as an economist, would strengthen the Center Union's reformist platform.

From Léopoldville, I wrote a congratulatory note to Andreas on the Center Union's long-sought victory and his own successful run for Parliament. I wasn't sure what he would make of his first term as a back bencher, but then he never was one. Instead, his father rashly appointed him to high (and ill-suited) ministerial positions that caused considerable resentment among senior Center Union deputies whom Andreas had leapfrogged over. The hostile atmosphere was evident in the summer of 1965 when Toni and I stopped in Athens en route to our next assignment in Washington DC. We were adopting a Greek baby, and since the final paperwork took most of a month, we saw both the older and younger Papandreous on several occasions.

Andreas greeted us as old friends, but his new friends struck me as a distinctly oily coterie. Their talk was filled with intrigue and allusions to political developments I knew nothing about. There were plenty of hints in the conservative press, where I read gleeful accounts of nefarious goings on: an affair between Andreas and the wife of one of his inner circle; a plot (called the ASPIDA affair) involving Andreas and a cadre of disgruntled army officers to purge royalist domination of the armed forces; growing rifts between father and son as Andreas pushed for more radical reforms; and even rumors of a tryst between George Papandreou and his daughter-in-law. Except for the last I should have taken the reports more seriously, but we were enjoying a holiday, a new baby, and the pleasant prospect of a home assignment after nearly eight years abroad.

Back in Washington we discovered television, practically unheard of in Léopoldville and Athens, which we turned on nightly to follow the news from Vietnam. The war was beginning to dominate the three major networks, as it was also much of my job as assistant to Averell Harriman, President Johnson's ambassador-at-large. A holdover from the Kennedy administration, Harriman had been given the futile task of setting up preliminary talks with the North Vietnamese, as well as mediating between the hawks and doves among Johnson's policy advisors.

With Vietnam occupying most of my attention I could barely keep up with the crises besetting the Center Union, and I was slow to grasp how much the patched-together government was unraveling.

Constantine Mitsotakis, the jilted heir to the party's leadership, formed an "Apostate" movement against George Papandreou, who was already in the midst of a dispute with the new king, Constantine, over his (Papandreou's) right to hold the minister of defense portfolio along with his premiership. Between the impasse with the king and rising dissensions within his party, Papandreou resigned. There followed a revolving door of temporary governments, street demonstrations, and persistent rumors of a military coup in the offing. Throughout, Andreas, who had become a vociferous opponent of his father's timid approach to reform, aroused fears among conservative voters that he was a communist at heart, leading the country into another civil war.

On April 21, 1967, while I was laid low in hospital with a chest infection, I turned on the television and was startled to see tanks surrounding the Parliament building on Syntagma Square. Within hours there were three Greek-born friends gathered around my bed, crying, "Monty! You must *do* something!" "Do what?" I thought through a medicated fog, "It's your problem." In 1968 I would hear directly about the coup from Andreas himself and eventually read full accounts of the cascade of events leading up to it in his *Democracy at Gunpoint* and Margaret's *Nightmare in Athens*, both published in the early 1970s.

For some months there had been numerous coup alerts that kept Andreas moving from place to place at night, but the putsch occurred during a period of relative calm, amid expectations that elections would still take place in May. Feeling safe, Andreas spent the night of April 20 at home, only to be awakened at 2 a.m. when a gang of armed soldiers burst through the front door. They proceeded to ransack every room, yelling "Where is he? Where is the traitor?" Margaret and her visiting father (a former marine) tried to fend them off, insisting that Andreas was not at home, while her mother, mother-in-law, and the three younger children tried to protect breakage in their bedrooms. At the same time, fourteen-year-old George was helping his father to elude the soldiers. They made their way up to a third-floor terrace, from which Andreas scrambled onto the roof. George crouched on the terrace, unsure what to do next, and was still there when the soldiers arrived and put a gun to his head. "Don't shoot!" Andreas implored, "I'm coming down." Gashing a knee as he jumped, he was allowed to dress and was then hauled away to prison and eight months of solitary confinement. Horrifying as those moments were, Andreas was only one of thousands rounded up that night, including George Papandreou and virtually all prominent politicians whether of the left, the center, or the right. Within a day the Junta had shut down the press, removed judges from the courts, and annulled eleven civil rights articles in the Constitution. Once again, Greece's fragile democracy had fallen to dictatorial rule.

As described in my introduction, by January 1968 Andreas had been released and was on his way to Sweden, where he had been offered a visiting lectureship by his friend and supporter, Prime Minister Olaf Palme. I was now in London, dealing principally with Anglo-American differences over the Biafran secession in Nigeria and Anglo-American agreement to keep to the timetable set for Northern Rhodesia's imminent independence, strenuously resisted by its last colonial prime minister, the thuggish white supremacist Ian Smith. As I was poring over Nigerian ethnicities—Hausa, Igbo, Yoruba—my office telephone rang. It was Margaret, calling to say that she and Andreas were passing through London and were we free to see them that evening? "Come for dinner," I replied, relying as usual on Toni to throw a meal together on short notice.

This was a bad habit. We now had three children under three. After adopting little Christopher, Toni gave birth to Jonathan in Washington in 1966 and to David in London in 1967. (A disapproving neighbor called them "Irish triplets.") Fortunately the Papandreous arrived an hour late, and only David's wails for his ten o'clock bottle interrupted our lengthy evening reunion.

Andreas was in an agitated state: thin, drinking too much, pacing the floor, and muttering repeatedly, "The Greeks have *betrayed* me." Days later, at a press conference in Stockholm, he changed "The Greeks" to "Anti-democratic imperialist forces," but that night I was not yet one of them and Andreas felt free to vent his feelings.

The best we could do was listen and try to encourage thoughts of a happier future. Silently, we pitied his misfortunes, however much of his own making, and when the evening ended, I had nothing to add except to wish them good health and Godspeed. He was finished, Toni and I agreed over pillow talk, neither of us imagining that Andreas's next incarnation was just beginning.

That was the last we saw of the Papandreous until 1974, although when George Papandreou died in November 1968, we did see British television coverage of his funeral procession. Andreas was not allowed to return, but Margaret was a prominent presence among thousands of mourners. Clambering onto her father-in-law's casket, she addressed the crowds in proficient Greek, promising them that Andreas's resistance movement would prevail in bringing democracy back to Greece. What came through to us was her passion for Andreas's cause and how clearly her own ambitions matched his.

By then the Papandreou family was in Toronto, where Andreas launched his Pan-Hellenic Liberation Movement (PAK). It gathered adherents from Greek exiles in both Europe and the United States, if not widespread coverage in the American media. Their focus was on Richard Nixon's victory over Hubert Humphrey in the November 1968 elections, the Vietnam War, and growing protests against it that used much of the same rhetoric and political criticism of United States government policies as Andreas's. He made impassioned speeches at dozens of academic conferences on the theme that American chicanery, particularly the CIA's, was responsible for the Colonels' regime. On two occasions, however, he also made national appearances on American television, once on NBC's panel news program *Meet the Press* in late 1968, and in 1972 on PBS's *Firing Line*, hosted by William F. Buckley. Reading the transcripts today, one is struck by the different planets the interviewers and Andreas inhabited. Virtually every question to him began with his position on communism, whether he was seeking alliances with communists in Greece or elsewhere and, by the way, hadn't he been a communist himself? To which Andreas steadfastly replied that he had been a Trotskyite, a far different term in the 1930s, and after living over twenty years in the United States he called him-self a proud New Dealer, a Democratic Socialist in the European sense, and an opponent of tyranny in every form. This allowed him to get back to America's pernicious role in the fall of democracy in Greece, at least briefly, before his interviewers again drove home the importance of the democracies keeping communism at bay. He fared better in Europe, particularly with the Scandinavian and French press, and he continued to swell PAK's enrollment with expa-triate Greeks, among them young technocrats—engineers, scien-tists, urban planners, and the like—whose skills Andreas hoped to introduce in Greece.

My London assignment was cut short when our newly appointed ambassador to Laos, previously our ambassador in Léopoldville, assembled his old Congo hands for his "country team," as senior staff members are called, and as deputy chief of mission I plunged into a supposedly neutral country helplessly caught up in the Vietnam War.

In 1973 I returned to Washington and became deputy assistant secretary for Asian affairs. With much of my time spent testifying before Congress on how to achieve a decent exit from Vietnam, I almost missed the news of a student uprising in Athens in Novem-ber of that year. It would mark the beginning of the end of the Col-onels' regime. In July 1974, while vacationing with Toni and the children on Cape Cod (four-year-old Emily now bravely bringing up the rear), I read fast-breaking news from Greece: the Junta's bun-gled attempt to overthrow Cypriot president archbishop Makarios ("The Red Priest," the Colonels had labeled him) followed by Tur-key's immediate invasion and occupation of the northern part of the island to protect its minority Turkish population. Greece was in a panic, and as the Junta collapsed the State Department sum-moned me back to Washington.

There I met with Henry Kissinger, who instructed me to depart posthaste for Athens. At first, I assumed that, as one who knew Greece—at least better than he—I was going on a temporary mis-sion to assess the situation. But no, my assignment was to hold down the fort as deputy chief of mission while Washington began a house cleaning of our embassy staff, some of it associated too closely with the fallen regime. Since an ambassador has the privilege of picking his own DCM, I balked at being parachuted into Athens without the current ambassador's approval. "Henry Tasca is a Republican donor and close personal friend of President Nixon," I argued my case, "he's just going to send me packing." "Don't worry," Kissinger growled curtly, "Tasca will be gone soon after you get there, and so will his friend." His prediction was off by a few weeks, perhaps understandably, given his joint responsibilities as secretary of state, national security advisor, and (it was widely reported) companion in prayer to Richard Nixon in the final weeks before his resignation.

Once the dust settled, I remained as DCM to the new ambassador, Jack Kubisch, an able chief of mission with whom I worked closely, albeit for less time than I had hoped. For my willingness to take up the Athens assignment at a lower level than my rank, I was rewarded with a promotion and an ambassadorship in West Africa. I had hoped for a lengthier stay, but this second tour packed as much action as my first and with more serious consequences for Greek-American relations.

7

The Post-Junta Scene

THE OFFICIAL COLORS of Greece are blue and white, from its national flag to passports, government seals, and Olympic athletes' uniforms. And well they should be for a land of blue sky and white marble, blue sea, whitewashed houses, and the talismanic blue evil eye that wards off danger. It came as something of a surprise, therefore, when Andreas Papandreou's newly formed socialist party (PASOK) launched itself under the banner of "The Green Sun," following his return to Athens in 1974, no longer an exile but a full-throated challenger to Greece's hidebound politics and social traditions.

The PASOK sun was a lush tropical green, more reminiscent of the Mayans than the Mediterranean. But green was chosen to signify rebirth, a break with the past, as did the party slogan of *"allaghi,"* or "change." It would be chanted from the rooftops as the liberated country geared up for the first election in over ten years.

As the Junta was rounded up for trial, its parting gesture was to relinquish power to a group of senior politicians, many of whom had been jailed, lived under house arrest, or fled the country. At the airport, thousands of Athenians greeted them with boisterous cheers. But the loudest cheers were for Constantine Karamanlis, whose reputation for skillful governance made him the inevitable choice to end the chaos the Junta had bequeathed the nation. After several days of jockeying behind closed doors his colleagues appointed him interim prime minister, a position he consolidated by handily winning the November 1974 elections.

Like Papandreou, Karamanlis also campaigned as a reformist, changing the conservative party's name from the Greek Radical Union (ERE) to New Democracy (ND). Trailing but gathering speed, PASOK gained a foothold in Parliament with 13.5 percent of the vote, a tally that would nearly double in 1977, and double again for a PASOK victory in 1981. From then on PASOK and ND were the only serious contenders in Greek politics.

Athenian sophisticates sniffed at PASOK's scruffy public image. While ND candidates campaigned in tailored suits and wingtip shoes, Andreas (as both his supporters and opponents called him) and his band of PASOK candidates dressed in jeans and motorcycle jackets. They dropped street slang into their speeches and hammered home their vow to sweep away all those politicians whose outdated platforms had long failed to address the contemporary needs of the Greek people. Among those whom PASOK consigned to the dust bin was Andreas's own father, once the beloved leader of Greece's political center. Old and enfeebled, and under house arrest until his death in 1968, George Papandreou died heartbroken by the demise of the democratic system and by the son who had turned against him. The Center Union carried on under George Mavros, a George Papandreou loyalist who took second place in the 1974 election but thereafter watched his party decline steadily against the forces of PASOK.

I recognized this decline as inevitable, but I remembered George Papandreou, warts and all, with a certain fondness. He was my introduction to Greek politics, and by observing their workings through both his eyes and his son's I felt I had some understanding of Andreas's ambition to supplant him. And knowing that this ambition was the wellspring of his conversion back to Greekness, and his need to prove it to his countrymen, gave me less concern about his anti-American campaign rhetoric than it did to most of the embassy staff.

Greeks *were* more skeptical of the United States' role in their internal affairs, most recently exemplified by the Nixon administration's tacit support of the Junta in exchange for its support of lucrative American business investments in Greece and granting home porting for our Sixth Fleet. That it had also been fascist and parochial, arresting citizens for "anarcho-communist" leanings, "anti-Christian" behavior, and "social depravity," was of no concern to the likes of Vice President Spiro Agnew, business magnates, and the Pentagon.

The truth was that the Cold War guided American foreign policy for over forty years, and our wink-and-a-nod relations with antidemocratic leaders, whether Arab potentates, African kleptocrats, or kowtowing South Vietnamese generals, had given the United States a reputation for backing any authoritarian regime, as long as it was anti-communist. By 1974 Greece was hardly endangered by creeping communism. EDA and other communist-infiltrated parties were already reduced to splinter groups, and in all subsequent elections would serve only as a protest vote for die-hard Stalinists and contrarian intellectuals.

The problem now was general hysteria over Turkey's invasion of Northern Cyprus, accompanied by a wave of national resentment against Washington's unwillingness to respond with military action of its own. Angry demonstrators burnt Kissinger in effigy and thousands marched weekly to the American embassy to denounce American treachery, ignoring, I should add, the Turkish embassy just across the street. We maintained a dignified posture until one group of demonstrators got out of hand, smashing windows and breaking into the consular offices and setting them on fire with petrol-soaked rags. The damage was extensive, and for the first time we had to take security measures that would utterly change the embassy's landmark architecture. Designed by Walter Gropius to symbolize the openness of American society, the square marble-and-glass building enclosed a spacious courtyard where ambassadors held the annual Fourth of July reception for hundreds of guests and the usual freeloaders, who strolled in through four entrances facing the sidewalks. Three had to be closed; the lone elderly guard we had greeted each morning for years was replaced by a squad of armed police; and the windows were smeared with an unsightly shatterproof gel. Then came concrete vehicle blocks and eventually a high wall around the entire compound, transforming our symbol of openness into Fortress America.

But before the fire, and however irritating the demonstrations, we felt no personal threat and considered that the main danger to life and limb was now the number of cars on the streets, their drivers hurtling at breakneck speed between traffic lights, or even racing through them, to the pedestrians' peril. A visiting cousin of mine from California ventured out on her own and returned ashen faced. "Don't they have *any* rules of the road around here?" she asked, collapsing on the sofa. "Or do they learn them on bumper cars at the amusement park?" Equally disagreeable to her impressions of Athens was the *nefos*, a yellowish-brown pancake smog caused by vehicular pollution that blotted out the sun for much of the summer and lingered until the winter rains.

In 1975 those rains brought a more serious peril—if not for the general population—with the appearance of Greece's first terrorist group, "17 November," the date of the failed student uprising against the Junta that had been put down with the loss of several lives. But 17 November was much more than a remnant anti-Junta group; it was a small but lethal gang of anarchic/leftist ideologues whose twisted goal was simply to kill anyone who represented any form of the establishment.

Their first victim was our CIA station chief, Richard Welch. To my everlasting regret, I had enthusiastically recommended him to Ambassador Kubisch precisely because he was the antithesis of what Greeks liked to call "the dark forces of foreign intrigue." A Harvard graduate with a degree in classics, Dick and I had served together in Athens on my first tour, and I admired his level-headed approach, at the height of the Cold War, to what the CIA should and shouldn't do in the name of democracy. Dick was a fluent Greek speaker and had also served in Cyprus. He leapt at the opportunity to return to his favorite part of the world. On December 23, 1975, he was shot dead by 17 November, outside his house as he returned from a Christmas party at the ambassador's residence. His premature death at age forty-four devastated his family and everyone who knew him. After all these years I still remember a line of Dick's handwritten note to me when he learned of his appointment: "Am still pinching myself for my good fortune!"

If there was any consolation to draw from Dick's assassination it was a law set in motion by Congress to criminalize disclosure of intelligence agents' identities—not that Dick wasn't known as a station chief to many Greeks who specialized in figuring out who was undercover at the embassy—but it did put a halt to a spate of tell-all books about CIA officers still on active duty. Sadly, for nearly thirty years 17 November would continue to mow down dozens of both Greeks and foreigners, and its notorious longevity would give PASOK its reputation as an indifferent guardian against domestic and international terrorism alike.

Before the onset of terrorism in Greece, however, our first concerns were more in the realm of public relations, principally to dissuade a significant portion of the Greek population from their lingering belief that American complicity had brought the Junta to power. That, of course, was Andreas's rallying cry, and he made the most of it. To his credit, Karamanlis didn't, and once the hoopla surrounding the Junta leaders' trials and imprisonment died down, he moved on as if they had scarcely existed. At the age of sixty-six, he knew that the time was short to achieve his lifelong goal to move Greece out of political instability and toward economic growth by integrating it more closely with Europe. To that end he held a referendum on the monarchy and oversaw the creation of a new constitution in accordance with the results; he relegitimized all political parties, called for an "adjustment" in Greece's security relationship with the United States, and began negotiating the terms that would allow Greece to join the Common Market, precursor of the European Union. It was hard work. "In this country," he once told me, "You don't just wind the clock; you have to push the hands around yourself."

The referendum took place in December 1974. While it was becoming clear that the Greeks would choose a republic over a monarchy, I thought it a generous gesture by Karamanlis to invite the exiled king to address the Greeks before the vote and address them again in a farewell speech to his dwindling number of supporters. More arduous were the negotiations over the Status of Forces Agreement (SOFA) with the United States, for which I was the lead negotiator in what both sides knew would be certain reductions in our military presence that would give the Greeks more say over our access to ports, air bases, and listening posts but leave the objectives of our security assistance intact. This being Greece, the negotiations were suspended, and then restarted when I returned to Athens in 1981.

Before turning the reins over to his ND successor in 1977, Karamanlis drew fire from both right and left by finessing calls to go to war with Turkey. It was militarily too strong, a fellow NATO member, and its occupation of Northern Cyprus now a fait accompli, to be resolved by diplomatic means, or the passage of time—as remained the case. The United Nations' buffer zone, or Green Line, separating the Republic of Cyprus from the Turkish Republic of Northern Cyprus is still there, and the latter is still recognized only by Turkey, on which it continues to depend for legitimacy as well as economic survival.

As I had expected, throughout my second tour in Athens Andreas kept a safe distance from the American embassy. He had also moved to Kastri and rented out the Guizi Street house Toni and I knew so well from friendlier days. Both he and Margaret made it clear to us that there would be no socializing. When our paths crossed at public events, we shook hands politely, inquired about our respective children, and went our separate ways. It was another paradox of Andreas's life that many Greek voters still questioned his Greekness, still thought of him as "O Amerikanos" and, worse, a betrayer of his adopted country. By avoiding American officialdom, he established his Greek credentials but was still American enough to raise funds for PASOK from "Limousine Liberals" in the United States. A further irony was that Margaret was an enthusiastic marcher in the demonstrations against the embassy, and her participation became the source of many jokes. (*"Well*, since I'm here I might as well renew my passport.") She too had to establish her Greek credentials, which she began to do by speaking out on feminist issues: civil marriage, abortion rights, access to birth control, childcare, and equal pay for Greece's increasing number of women joining the work force. The jump in the number of women voting for PASOK in 1977 proved her efforts were paying off.

By that time I was following PASOK's dramatic rise from the vantage point of the calm political atmosphere of West Africa's most prosperous county, the Ivory Coast. Unlike the Congo, my second African tour was a peaceful one. Our interests were mostly commercial and our influence a distant second to the French, whose ambassador was a rotund proconsul and seemingly permanent dean of the diplomatic corps. The country's first and highly esteemed president was Félix Houphuët-Boigny, who had been a prominent tribal chief and planter before entering politics when the Ivory Coast was still a colony. He had served many years as an *outre-mer* (overseas) deputy in the French Parliament and held several ministerial positions before the Ivory Coast's independence in 1960. Houphuët-Boigny was considered a political moderate, confirmed anti-communist, and well disposed toward the Western Alliance.

My time in Abidjan corresponded with a period of economic prosperity derived largely from coffee and cocoa exports, a thriving tourist industry, and a huge number of French advisors and technocrats employed by the Ivorian government. Abidjan's modernity was luxurious by African standards, with glass air-conditioned office buildings, French restaurants, and even a skating rink off the lobby of the state-of-the-art Hotel Ivoire. Swimming pools dotted the gardens in Cocody, an upper-class suburb reached by a winding corniche and marginally cooler than downtown. The American embassy residence was there, a tastefully furnished villa with ample bedrooms for children and guests and a thatched gazebo at one end of the pool to remind us we were in Africa.

My days were busy, but not overburdened, and in these steamy but serene surroundings Toni and I belatedly read *Democracy at*

Gunpoint and *Nightmare in Athens*, in the process reliving all the extraordinary events that had befallen the Papandreous since those halcyon days when we were neighbors and friends, two American couples swapping impressions of "our Greek experience." When Toni and I talked about Greece, it was as of a place behind us, a place we'd visit some distant day on a vacation. We'd had our turn, two turns in fact, but who'd ever heard of three?

8

Prime Time

AFTER THREE YEARS in the Ivory Coast I returned to Washington to serve as vice president of our National Defense University, a mid-career training institute for both military and Foreign Service officers who studied together for a year and emerged with a greater and valuable understanding of each other's professions. In the spring of 1981, I was leading a group of them on a two-week tour of Eastern Europe when a telephone call from the White House reached me in Budapest.

Ronald Reagan had been president for two months, and his administration was doling out ambassadorships to his campaign contributors. The largest, most luxurious capitals (or the easygoing Caribbean ones) were almost always reserved for political friends, and they were usually paired with an experienced Foreign Service officer to serve as deputy chief of mission. With Greece now fully integrated into the State Department's prestigious Bureau of European Affairs, our Athens embassy might well have appealed to one of the Reagans' inner circle, but I suspect that Greece's mercurial political scene helped the State Department persuade the administration that an old Greek hand would have a firmer grasp of events than a California business mogul. I also suspect that the president knew absolutely nothing about me, but with his cue cards in front of him he greeted me over the phone as a fellow Californian and said affably, "How'd you like to be my man in Athens?"

I said I was honored by his request but would, of course, have to consult my wife. I hung up, immediately called Toni, and announced in no uncertain terms that I was taking the job. She wasn't that surprised by the offer, having already gotten wind of it in the European Affairs bureau and had actually heard from the White House before I did. Somewhat to her embarrassment, she was doing laundry and thought the call was from an old friend and colleague, Charlie Whitehouse. "Hold on a minute, Charlie, the spin cycle's off balance," she told an irritated operator, who then asked to have my whereabouts spelled out: "*B* as in boy," she began, "*D* as in doctor . . ." "*P* as in pest," the operator finished angrily. "Speaking of which," Toni reminded me when I returned to Washington, "we have to enroll in the Ambassadorial Charm School."

This was a three-day seminar for neophyte appointments, but included Foreign Service officers as well, mostly for updates on security, new office tools (Speakerphones! Wang computers!) and a new Art for Embassies program that enabled us to borrow works from American museums and artists' private collections to display in residences and chanceries. Toni and I knew the Athens residence well and took great pleasure selecting paintings and sculpture suited to its spacious reception rooms. The rest of the briefings I paid only pro forma attention to, believing that a secretary would cope with the Wang and that I could put my foot down over too restrictive security measures. (There would be much gnashing of teeth on both counts.)

Although it was high summer when we arrived, the October 1981 election campaign was boisterously underway. Karamanlis, now elevated to the presidency, had been succeeded by George Rallis as leader of New Democracy. A man of great courage and integrity, he was, however, less charismatic than his predecessor and his platform, necessarily based on "continued prosperity and normalcy," lacked the excitement of PASOK's relentless cries for "*Allaghi!*" "Out of NATO!" and "Greece for the Greeks!"

While my courtesy call on President Karamanlis was devoted largely to the still-unresolved question of how and whether Turkish troops might be removed from Cyprus, my call on George Rallis was a candid discussion of the upcoming elections and New Democracy's prospects of staying in power. Rallis had his doubts, and these were reinforced by his pessimistic and bluntly outspoken wife, Lena, when Toni called on her a few days later at their Athens apartment. As they chatted over lemonade, a seemingly endless stream of PASOK marchers chanting "*Allaghi!*" on the street below drowned out their conversation. Exasperated, Lena Rallis got up, closed the shutters, and muttered, "I tell you, Toni, we are *feenished* this time, *feenished*. I tell you that if *God* came down from Heaven, he would vote PASOK."

Toni's report notwithstanding, my own assessment of the country's mood was mixed. I still thought that Andreas's wild rhetoric risked alienating a sufficient number of voters for New Democracy to prevail; on the other hand, seven years of conservative rule had left ND somewhat stale and exhausted. Since this election pitted continuity versus change, the question was whether there were enough disaffected Greeks to accept Papandreou's extreme version of the latter. In my reports to Washington I predicted that Rallis would edge out Papandreou by the thinnest of margins, but I now think that my estimate was influenced by a desire not to alarm Washington, where Andreas was regarded as a dangerous figure by many powerful factions, and where my long acquaintance with him made me suspect among certain conservative Greek Americans who had objected to my appointment to Athens. My first-rate political section heartily disagreed, and of course they were right. On October 18, PASOK won over 48 percent of the vote and a comfortable majority of 172 parliamentary seats, leaving New Democracy and a divided communist party with respectively 36 percent and 12 percent of the electoral vote. For the first time in Greece's history, a socialist government had come to power, pledging to free Greece from American "imperialism" and forced membership in the NATO alliance.

With the change of prime ministers, it was customary for all ambassadors in Athens to request a courtesy call on the victor, and the order in which it was granted was usually a sign of their countries' standing with the new government. Given the demonic role the United States had played during PASOK's electoral campaign, I thought it best to delay my request for a meeting with Andreas and waited several weeks before making it. The first ambassadors he received were from the Arab states, followed by Yugoslavia, whose nonaligned foreign policies Andreas had long touted as a model for Greece. Ambassadors from the NATO states were pushed down the line, and when my turn came, I noted that the date coincided with the beginning of a three-day holiday, and the hour, well after dark. On very short notice I was summoned to call on Papandreou in his parliamentary office on Syntagma Square.

Formerly the royal palace, the Greek parliament was built in neo-classical style by nineteenth-century German architects whose other public buildings in the heart of Athens always gave me the sense of being half in Berlin and half in the Balkans. When the Greeks converted the palace into a legislative assembly, rabbit warrens of offices sprang up around the deputies' chamber, and a rear entrance became the standard way to reach them without having to cross the vast plaza to the ceremonial front one. With some foreboding about my first private encounter with Andreas in several years, augmented by the fact that the building was closed and pitch-dark for the holiday, I stepped into the labyrinthine corridors and was escorted by a solitary guard up to the prime minister's office suite. The door was slightly ajar, and I could see what appeared to be a glare of klieg lights inside.

My first thought was that I had been booby trapped, that Andreas was going to launch into a litany of grievances against the United States, and that I was to be the butt of his denunciations. I was right about the klieg lights. A swarm of Greek and international reporters and photographers crowded the room, through which Andreas made his way toward me, with an outstretched hand and a wry smile on his face. After a brief comment to the domestic press he switched to English for the international one and then complimented me on my return. We had known each other a long time, he continued, putting an arm over my shoulder, and he was confident that relations between our two countries would stay on an even keel.

Unprepared for the publicity, I responded with what I hoped was the right combination of optimism and ambiguity, relieved by his cordial welcome but not wanting to sound like an acolyte. After shaking hands with me for the cameras, Papandreou dismissed the press, and I turned to follow in their wake. "Wait a minute!" he called out. "Let's have a drink before you go." We sat down in two battered leather armchairs in front of his desk and over whiskey and sodas we fell silent for a moment until Andreas raised his glass and said exactly what had been running through my mind as well.

"Tell me, Monty," he said, breaking into a broad grin, "twenty years ago, in your wildest dreams, would you ever have thought that *I* would be sitting in this chair, and *you* in that one?"

No, I hadn't, although it now seemed the logical outcome of our strangely overlapping lives. But pleasantries over drinks scarcely addressed the serious foreign policy differences between the Papandreou and Reagan administrations, administrations that instinctively distrusted each other and had totally opposing views on America's proper role in the world. While I understood the history behind Andreas's castigation of our over-militarized approach to Greece, an approach too narrowly defined by the exigencies of the Cold War, I found his public stance against everything the United States stood for cynically overblown and counterproductive. Over the next four years Andreas would soften his tone with me and with visiting American officials, if not with the hard-left ministers in his cabinet. Explaining to Washington what Papandreou was all about became a major undertaking.

This may be the appropriate place to comment on another aspect of ambassadors' jobs, particularly American ambassadors', and on Washington's increasingly held view that a chief of mission's task is simply to carry out instructions. My career began in the days when the State Department still developed cadres of officers with particular expertise in a country or region: Sovietologists, Arabists, Sinologists, and the like, and these valuable skills enabled them to guide policy as well as carry it out. That said, an envoy's reputation could be damaged by charges of "localitis," the insidious sin of becoming too partial to a host country's point of view and losing one's objectivity in the process. Eminent American envoys, starting with Benjamin Franklin in Paris and including George Kennan in Moscow, were accused of localitis: Franklin, for basking in the attention of the French Court, and Kennan, for his profound grasp of Russian culture and history that led to his "Long Telegram" advising containment over saber-rattling. Kennan left the Foreign Service prematurely, but fortunately his containment policy, with some exceptions, was largely adopted.

In my own case, suspicions of localitis had been raised during my confirmation hearing, not least by a prominent Greek shipowner, who expressed his concern to Secretary of State Alexander Haig that I had been too close to Andreas Papandreou, and to his father. He cited a passage from Margaret Papandreou's book, *Nightmare in Athens*, in which she reprints the congratulatory note I sent from the Congo to the elder Papandreou after the 1963 Greek elections. Although by now I had served in a variety of posts, it was common knowledge that Toni and I had already served two tours in Athens, spoke Greek, enjoyed the Greek way of life, and knew most of the political figures still active on the scene. When the secretary questioned me about the shipowner's charges, I replied that I was going to Athens to represent the United States in Greece, not the other way around, and he let the matter rest. Nonetheless, I was aware that the issue could arise again if Papandreou seemed to be having his way with a presumably gullible American envoy.

As it happened, the PASOK government's first contretemps was not with Washington but with Karamanlis, and it was purely sartorial in nature. When the Greek president scheduled his customary reception to introduce the diplomatic corps to the new government, the invitations specified black tie, a tradition that went against PASOK's determinedly proletarian dress code. After much negotiating, the impasse was broken when both sides grudgingly agreed to wear business suits, and even then, some PASOK deputies showed up without neckties. (I note that the style has become de rigueur among political leaders today.)

Abroad, Andreas soon faced similar compromises. For symbolic and practical purposes (and like his father before him) he had assumed the position of minister of defense and in that capacity was preparing to attend his first NATO conference in Spain. Shortly before his departure, he summoned me on "a matter of some urgency" to his home, his father's former villa in Kastri and scarcely changed from the days Toni and I had first visited it. I steeled myself for an announcement that he was going to break ranks with NATO. Instead I found him staring at the conference schedule and wondering if he would need formal evening wear at the opening dinner. When I told him it was customary, Andreas broke into a sweat and asked for the name of a good tailor. I put him in touch with one I had used myself, and Andreas was properly fitted out in time, but I never told him I had gotten the tailor's name from his predecessor George Rallis and had to plead Andreas's case before the tailor agreed to do business with "that damn socialist." My behind-the-scenes diplomacy boosted Andreas's appearance at the NATO gathering but not his reputation when he became the first and only member to veto the joint statement of purpose that always ended the gatherings. No statement was issued, although over the years Andreas would fudge the time frame for Greece's withdrawal from the alliance.

Our bilateral military exchanges endured the same slights. In early 1982 the commander of the Sixth Fleet paid an official visit to Athens, at the end of which I hosted a stag dinner. Papandreou sent his deputy defense minister, who attended only on the condition that there would be no exchange of toasts and no public recognition of Greek-American military cooperation—never mind that that was the point of the admiral's visit, or that Greek military officials had raised no objections to said cooperation or to the presence of American military bases on the mainland and the island of Crete. Such gratuitous insults, issued to satisfy the party faithful, did nothing to enhance PASOK's reputation in Washington or in the admiral's CINCSOUTH headquarters in Naples.

Secretary of State Haig fared somewhat better during his only visit to Athens that spring. As a former supreme commander of NATO he understood the delicate balance we would have to maintain with the new PASOK government (a balance he failed to achieve with his own department or cabinet colleagues in Washington, who would soon spearhead his early resignation). Sensing Haig's high opinion of himself, Papandreou flattered his guest, advising his staff "to close their briefing books, because Secretary Haig knows the issues better than anyone else in this meeting." Haig was indeed seduced by Papandreou, and on the drive back from an informal dinner in Kastri (served not by uniformed butlers but a housekeeper in slippers) he told me how "much more reasonable and flexible" the prime minister had turned out to be—a compliment I was to hear often when Andreas reverted to his chin-stroking, sagacious statesman's persona.

His handling of the Haig visit was an early indication that Papandreou intended to keep politico-military relations with the United States in his own hands, and so he often communicated with me in private before or after meetings with his subordinates in his defense and foreign affairs ministries. On one occasion he summoned me to his office to discuss, over wine and cheese, his intention to name Karolos Papoulias as minister of foreign affairs. Papoulias spoke no English, and Andreas wanted my opinion on whether this deficiency would handicap him in his job. I reassured him that there were plenty of foreign ministers who dealt with other governments through interpreters, and Papoulias (who later became president of the Greek Republic) went on to be an effective and pragmatic minister, more interested in solving problems than scoring political points.

Other members of Papandreou's cabinet made life more difficult, starting with the first two ministers for education and religious affairs, both of whom were hell-bent on eliminating the "elitist" American-sponsored private schools in Greece, of which there were now several, one or two offering university degrees as well as high school diplomas. The most prominent were Athens College and Anatolia College in Thessaloniki, established even earlier than Athens College by Protestant missionaries for Greek refugee children fleeing the Smyrna disaster in Turkey in 1922. By the 1970s Greek students who could not afford to study abroad were flocking to new American postsecondary institutions offering both liberal arts and business-oriented degrees more progressive and career-oriented than the rigid curriculum prevailing in Greece's state universities.

Quite early on, officials in the Ministry of Education began to harass the American schools, threatening restrictions on the curriculum, harsh administrative rules, ruinous taxes, and the expulsion of undesirable teachers. One such "undesirable" taught a model United Nations course, in which students were assigned to represent a nation, research its foreign policy positions, and present them to the class, playing the part of the General Assembly. When a resolution over the Turks' occupation of Northern Cyprus called for one student to represent Turkey and another the United States, the ministry reacted by vilifying the unfortunate teacher in the press, to the point that, after vain efforts to halt the attacks on himself and his family, he eventually left in despair. On this and several other instances I gave up trying to reason with the Ministry of Education and went directly to Andreas to protest. The essence of his reply was that while he could not contradict PASOK's official opposition to private schools in general, he could assure me that the government would not shut them down. He claimed that PASOK's goal was to harmonize them with the national education system: equivalency of degrees, ratio of foreign board members to Greek ones, course material, and so on. When I relayed this information to the American directors, however, they were justifiably skeptical, and throughout my term as U.S. ambassador I had to repeatedly intervene on their behalf. Despite the hostile atmosphere, and many tweaks to their status, the schools remain open to this day. And with the growth of other foreign university programs throughout the country, there is now an alliance of international schools in Greece.

Today, of course, between the Euro monetary system and pan-European access to university degrees, Greek students have many options to pursue a foreign one, but I note that as recently as a few years ago the EU was still pressuring the Greek government to recognize foreign diplomas and not restrict Greek graduates holding them from entering certain professions (among them the civil service and teaching). Another factor that may ensure the continuation of foreign schools is Greece's changing population. For centuries Greece was a homogenous society based on one language and one religion. Today, between globalization and immigration, it is awash with non-Greeks, legal or otherwise, from Chinese entrepreneurs (who now own the Port of Piraeus) to desperate Middle Eastern and African refugees fleeing wars or famine in their homelands. This influx of foreigners, many of whom may never become—or want to become—Greek citizens, argues the case for even more international schools in the future.

The Ministry of Labor was equally unhelpful in working with us to restrain striking employees from blocking access to Hellenikon, our military airbase on the outskirts of Athens. The irony of the strikers' conflicting objectives—on the one hand to close the base, on the other to be paid higher wages—reflected the political divide in the union itself (its leader was a former Junta supporter) and created one very messy scene at the entrance gate. For months it was littered with tents, sleeping bags, placards, and trash while the labor minister ignored the situation, and personnel had to negotiate their way inside through a hail of pounding fists on their car windows.

In contrast, the minister of urban planning, Antonis Tritsis, who was married to an American and had taught in the United States, drew readily on American expertise to conduct a cadastral survey of the Athens area and to recommend methods to reduce air pollution. A delightful man to know and to work with, Tritsis went on to become minister of education and mayor of Athens. Sadly, he died far too young of a stroke in 1992.

I also enjoyed a warm, if sometimes chaotic, friendship with the minister of culture, Melina Mercouri, the internationally acclaimed actress and political activist, passionate Junta resister and equally passionate advocate for the return of the Elgin Marbles to Greece. Both the Junta and the American government had made life difficult for her: in exile from the regime she lost her passport and her property, and after winning a parliamentary seat as a PASOK deputy in 1974 she was placed on the State Department's cautionary list of visa applicants. Each time she traveled to the United States she had to reapply, even though her husband was the Brooklyn-born film director Jules "Julie" Dassin. He, too, became a friend and backup keeper of his wife's appointment calendar when her disorganized office lost track of her schedule or whereabouts. Even her telephone was constantly out of order and once, when she and I were meeting in my office, she looked at the three phones on my desk and said, "Could I *please* have one of them?"

Melina and I worked together on Greece's cultural contribution to the 1984 Olympic Games in Los Angeles. Forgoing the folk dancing and craft exhibits that smaller, financially strapped nations usually offered the host city before the games got underway, we pushed for a performance of *Oedipus Rex*, persuading each other that it was sure to draw an audience of Hollywood psychiatrists and their patients. I'm not sure that it did, but Melina continued to show up faithfully at American cultural events in Athens—and was always a larger-than-life seat companion who put anyone next to her in the shade. She had a throaty laugh and a self-deprecating sense of humor that was on full display when we found ourselves together at a fur traders' exposition in the northern city of Kastoria. Both Toni and Melina were mobbed by sales representatives to sample their fur coats before the cameras, which Toni did discreetly before stepping back to let Melina strut her stuff. She selected the most luxurious, ankle-length mink from a rack and caressed it as she slipped it on for a model's walk around the showroom. Then she let the mink fall to the floor and trailed it behind her with one hand. "So bee-yoo-ti-ful!" she cooed, stroking the coat and turning full face to the cameras, "What a *pity* I'm a socialist."

As at the Ministry of Urban Planning, the new Ministry of the Environment was also stocked with Greeks who had studied environmental issues abroad. With Papandreou's encouragement we collaborated in their first efforts to reduce air and sea pollution. But we couldn't perform miracles. One summer almost the entire Greek coastline suffered an infestation of jellyfish so severe that when a swarm attacked Margaret Papandreou, she fell into a coma and nearly died from toxic shock. The tourist trade plummeted that year, and Andreas was so worried that he summoned a Marine biologist from the Chesapeake Bay to repel the invasion. I learned a lot about jellyfish from him, including the unfortunate truth that their appearance is always random, depending on sea currents, and that the only solution is patience until the currents change. While this was a frustrating response for Papandreou and disappointed bathers, it did put to rest assertions in the press that the Sixth Fleet was the culprit, allegedly attracting the jellyfish armada while roaming the Mediterranean and throwing trash overboard. On the contrary, the American navy followed far stricter sanitation regulations than did the Greeks, military or civilian, most of whom treated the Aegean as a bottomless garbage pail.

But this fairly calm working relationship that we established with the new government had its counter effects. Angry leftists believed that American imperialism had not abated in the slightest and was subverting the "Greece for the Greeks!" principles of the PASOK movement; angry rightists believed that Papandreou was a fellow traveler whose aim was to align Greece with the Soviet Bloc, as evidenced by his early visit to communist Poland, recently subjected to martial law by the hardline General Wojciech Jaruzelski and his Military Council of National Salvation. One CIA report of an imminent right-wing coup against Papandreou was so detailed in its particulars that I immediately passed it on to Andreas, who thanked me and then promptly invited Toni and me to dinner in Kastri on the supposed date of the coup. The gesture may have been his way of testing whether the American ambassador and the CIA station chief were using the same playbook. He still harbored a conspiratorial belief that the CIA conducted its own foreign policy in Greece and that presenting him with rumors of a coup was just a typical example of trying to put pressure on him. This belief was a constant in Papandreou's mind, dating back to his disappointment when the Kennedy administration, so many of whose members he had expected to support a populist uprising in Greece, had failed to follow through and heeded CIA alarmism instead. There was no way to dissuade him on this and other interpretations of CIA activities, which Kennedy had actually curtailed after the failed Bay of Pigs invasion in Cuba, giving absolute authority over the agency to American ambassadors abroad. Upon further investigation of my own station chief's report, I decided that the threat was not that imminent, and on the fateful evening Toni and I had a quiet dinner with the Papandreous, uninterrupted by right-wing extremists bursting through the door.

Meanwhile, left-wing fanatics were a decidedly tangible threat against Americans and had been since Dick Welch's assassination in 1975. Security considerations now put a great damper on how one moved about outside the embassy walls. Gone were the carefree days of our first tour in Athens when the only dangers Toni and I faced were falling off a fishing boat or confronting an angry goat on a mountain track. Toni and I explored Greece on foot, by car, and on island ferries. Now I was chauffeured around—in congested traffic—with a bodyguard on the lookout, because the 17 November gang used motorcycles to pull up alongside a target vehicle and fire at point-blank range.

Varying my hours and my travel routes was a limited option. The residence was on a one-way street, and many of my engagements were public by nature. Stepping out of my official car at a government or diplomatic function was the moment I always felt the most vulnerable, protected as I was by a security detail of revolving bodyguards and policemen in a follow car. Being Greek, they were highly personable and quickly became extended members of the family. At home, our adolescent children hung out with them far more than with us, picking up street slang and sex education as they kicked a soccer ball around the driveway. When I went gift shopping for Toni they felt personally invested in the purchase. "No, *no*, Mr. Ambassador, not the yellow negligee. The blue suits her so much better," and they were usually right.

This being our third assignment to Athens we had many old friends whom we preferred to see without our burly entourage, and for these private get-togethers we sometimes drove ourselves in a small car with Greek license plates. Once or twice we even slipped out the back gate and went to the movies in jeans and T-shirts. But such outings were rare, and for the most part, like our ambassadorial colleagues, we moved about with all our official baggage on display.

Our one genuine brush with danger occurred while most of Athens was asleep. On a rainy spring night, around 2 a.m., Toni and I were jolted awake by a deafening blast outside our bedroom window. There was an eerie silence, then the sound of footsteps scurrying on the gravel driveway and shouts of "A bomb! A bomb!" from the night guards at the gate. From the window we could see a smoldering, giant-sized hole in the wall facing the street and blown-out windows in the wing of the residence that abutted it—the wing in which three of our children, a houseguest, and two live-in servants were sleeping. They took the brunt of the explosion, which blanketed their rooms in shattered glass and wall plaster. By the time we had helped them pick their way over the shards to the rear of the second floor, the street was swarming with police and security men. Fortunately, no one was injured by the blast, but it was unsettling to realize that terrorists had no compunction about targeting a whole family, not just an individual.

There was considerable media coverage of the incident but I received no calls from the Ministry of Public Order to assure me they were taking the matter seriously. The next day, as a massive cleanup began, we went ahead with a previously scheduled reception for a visiting group from the National War College in Washington. When it was over, I still had received no word from a single Greek government official. Some hours later, as I sat in the library, pondering how to prod the authorities into action, the telephone rang. It was Andreas, calling anxiously (and rather belatedly, I thought) to say that a bomb had been discovered at the residence. In a huff I told him we were well aware of the fact and were sweeping up the debris, but he cut me off. "No, no! Not that bomb! There's a *second* bomb, at the back of your property. The detonation squad is working on it now. Don't go outside until you receive the all-clear."

I ignored his injunction and headed straight to the bottom of the garden. An army truck was pulling away from the back gate, and the guard stationed there pointed excitedly to a drainpipe that ran from a clay tennis court under the back wall to the street. The bomb had been wedged into the pipe, probably at the same time as the one hung on the front wall, and presumably set to go off at the same time. Perhaps because of the unseasonable rain it had not, and the next night the perpetrators returned to retrieve it. Spotting two men pulling up on a motor scooter and observing one of them poking into the open drain, the guard had challenged them and they sped off. The explosive proved to be a powerful one, but timed by an unreliable East German watch.

We were lucky. Three of my colleagues were not: our aforementioned Dick Welch, killed in 1975; U.S. Navy captain George Tsantes of the Joint U.S. Military Aid Group in 1983; and Defense Attaché William Nordeen, also a navy captain, in 1988. A fourth American target of 17 November miraculously—and bravely—managed to swerve his car as the terrorists fired through the window, and although badly wounded he kept driving to Hellenikon Air Base where he was employed, and was still collected enough to give some salient details about his assailants. We passed them on immediately. Yet PASOK chose to sweep the existence of 17 November under the rug or to lamely excuse its malevolent acts as understandable ones of grievance. In all, the group assassinated some two dozen Greeks and foreigners, and twenty-seven years would pass before all the gang members were captured. To this shameful story I can only offer my lifelong condolences to the Welch, Tsantes, and Nordeen families, all of whom came to Greece with best intentions and left overcome by grief.

During these years, terrorist agents of the Palestine Liberation Organization were also operating in Greece and caused further alarm by Papandreou's early embrace of Yassir Arafat, the first leader he invited to pay an official visit to Greece. Although the visit was purely ceremonial, it was part of Andreas's desire to associate Greece with the Non-Aligned Movement. He was one of the "group of six," including

Olaf Palme of Sweden and Indira Gandhi of India, seeking to ease tensions between East and West, and he later joined forces with Romania, a member of the Warsaw Pact, to promote the idea of a nuclear-free zone in the Balkans. There was little of substance to these proclamations, just as there was no follow-up on Andreas's insistence that Greece was about to withdraw from NATO and the European Union. Instead, he embarked on tactical retreats, claiming (rightly) that leaving the EU would be too damaging to the Greek economy and that logistical issues prevented a speedy exit from NATO.[1]

But one issue that could not be evaded or indefinitely postponed was the presence of American military bases on Greek soil. They were the product of our bilateral security agreement dating back to the Truman Doctrine, and their proximity to the Near East made them essential stepping-stones for communications, resupply, and transport needs in that troubled region. In addition to the main supply base at Hellenikon, there were communications stations at Marathon on the Attic Peninsula and on the island of Crete. Also on Crete was our naval base at Souda Bay, which was designated a NATO facility and was used both by the United States and its alliance partners.

Renegotiation of the existing agreement had begun with the previous Greek government but had never been completed. The Status of Forces Agreement (SOFA) under which American military personnel are allowed to operate in a host country has always been a bone of contention wherever those forces are stationed and whatever the host countries' governments, even the most conservative ones. At heart is the question of national sovereignty: namely, whether American bases abroad are subject to the host country's judicial, property, and labor laws that may differ considerably from American military ones. In the case of Greece, any agreement on those laws, and on the bases' continued existence, could be renegotiated at the government's choosing—and in the case of PASOK, its major goal was to close the bases completely.

The first round over the "Bases of Death," as demonstrators liked to call them, began in the fall of 1982, and as the two sides assembled their specialists I had to decide whether our negotiating team should be made up of insiders from our embassy or outsiders from Washington. It was tempting to keep direct responsibility and control from within; alternatively, if outside negotiators handled the daily give-and-take at the bargaining table it would free the embassy to intervene at a higher level if deadlocks developed. My experience as the lead negotiator in the suspended 1975 base talks led me to choose the latter option. The fact that Papandreou had already made clear his intention to consult with me as the talks progressed seemed an indication that he and I would have to soften the most recalcitrant delegates behind the scenes. To avoid the risk of intramural clashes between Washington and the embassy, I appointed my deputy chief of mission Alan Berlind, a politico-military specialist, as deputy to the lead Washington negotiator, Reginald Bartholomew. This arrangement worked fairly well, although there were times that Alan had to outdo Sisyphus, pushing not one but two boulders simultaneously up the mountain.

Bartholomew, who had been director of the State Department's Office of Politico-Military Affairs, and would later serve as ambassador to Lebanon, Spain, and Italy, was a tough-minded bargainer whose grasp of security issues far exceeded those of his Greek counterpart, Yannis Kapsis, the former editor of a left-leaning tabloid that had hysterically supported PASOK since 1974. What Kapsis did possess was a canny ability to drum up public anti-American sentiment through fear-mongering headlines and photographs. When I was DCM, he ran one of the latter purporting to show our marine guards mounting machine guns on the embassy roof, the better to shoot down Greek demonstrators. The fuzzy-looking machine guns in the photograph were actually stands for security cameras, common to most public buildings, but when I invited Kapsis to inspect the roof and bring photographers along, he sneered at the offer, on the grounds that of course we would remove the weapons first.

Laborious as the base negotiations were, the fact that Greece had not withdrawn from NATO worked in our favor, since many particulars of the SOFA agreements were now uniform throughout the

NATO alliance and changes to them would wreak havoc among its other members. For their part, the Greek negotiators insisted that any references to NATO appear only in the small print and that the main body of the text reflect PASOK's objective to shut down the bases within five years.

With the end of the Cold War still far from view, the American side—however aware that no military pact exists in perpetuity—wanted wording that was less explicit. As one of our negotiators put it, "We can't accept an agreement that, after five years, simply runs off a cliff." In the summer of 1983 the talks ground to a halt over the single verb "terminate."

The moment had come to sit down with the prime minister and discuss the linguistic nuances required for both sides to claim a satisfactory outcome. Contrary to his public rhetoric ("The bases must go!") I found Papandreou as anxious as I to get the negotiations over and done with, as long as the impression that PASOK had achieved its goal remained. The English-language version of the termination clause read that the agreement was "terminable" (i.e., "can be terminated") upon written notification by either one of the parties at least five months in advance. With his impeccable grasp of both languages, Andreas accepted the five-month notification clause that prevented the agreement from "running off a cliff" but insisted that the ambiguous use of "terminable" in English be replaced with the explicit "terminate" in Greek. And so, on this subtle compromise, the five-year base agreement was signed by both sides in the fall of 1983. To the best of my knowledge, it is the only one in which the wording of a critical clause is not identically rendered in both languages.

While the agreement hardly raised ripples among the American public, in Greece party stalwarts greeted it as a triumph, as "a treaty of departure, not continuation," and Papandreou's popularity reached new heights. As it turned out, however, neither the terminate/terminable clause of the treaty nor the advance notification requirement was ever put to the test. Changing circumstances and the passage of time led the United States to dismantle most of its bases in Greece before the five-year timetable was up, although because PASOK's pledge to withdraw from NATO was never carried out, the NATO naval base at Souda Bay remains open to this day.

But throughout my four-plus years as ambassador in Athens PASOK remained the bad boy of the alliance, using historical grievances against Turkey to continuously disrupt joint NATO exercises in the Aegean. In one 1983 exercise, the government refused to participate because the northeastern island of Limnos, a stone's throw from Turkey, was excluded. The island's status had long been disputed by the two countries, with Turkey contending that Limnos had been officially demilitarized by the Treaty of Lausanne in 1923 but that in subsequent years the Greeks had illegally remilitarized it, for obvious reasons. The PASOK government countered that in 1936, when the Montreux Convention revised the status of the Dardanelle Straits, the Turkish foreign minister had specifically excluded Limnos from the demilitarization provisions of the Lausanne Treaty. From then on, all Greek governments acted in the belief that the island's fortifications were completely legitimate.

The exercises were canceled, to the extreme annoyance of Washington and the commanders of the Sixth Fleet, but since Turkey had officially acquiesced to Limnos's remilitarization nearly fifty years before, I thought the Greeks had a valid case. I also thought that the Reagan administration might welcome Limnos's inclusion, in the interest of conducting future NATO exercises with PASOK's blessing, putting an end to the squabbling that characterized our security relationship with each other. While there was no possibility of Papandreou paying an official call on President Reagan, I sounded out the prime minister on the prospect of a low-key working visit with Defense Department officials, and he was quite receptive to the idea. While on home leave in August 1983, I pursued the matter further with the State Department and was reasonably optimistic until the first week of September, when the Soviets shot down a South Korean jumbo jet, killing hundreds of passengers, including an American congressman. As the rest of the NATO alliance—indeed most of the world—registered its outrage, Papandreou immediately defended the Soviets' claim that the jet was on a secret spy mission over Soviet territory and that they had shot it down in self-defense. Andreas's hasty and ill-considered statement of support for the Soviets promptly squelched any possibility of a visit to Washington, and my next call on him was an extremely prickly one.

Cutting short the usual pleasantries I expressed official and personal dismay that he could justify such a tragedy without the slightest evidence that the passenger jet was on anything but a routine flight. I took issue with his equally outlandish statement that if a Turkish aircraft had penetrated Greek airspace, he would have done just what the Soviets did and ordered the plane shot down. This was patently false. Despite several incidents of such penetration by the Turks, at no time had he given such an order—and these incidents involved military aircraft, not civilian ones.

Andreas was visibly uncomfortable but defended his support of the Soviets by claiming that it was no different from the position taken by some news organizations in the United States. "Such as?" I asked. He fumbled around and produced a lone example: an article in the *Nation*, which suggested that the Korean jumbo must have been a spy plane, probably in the CIA's employ, or why was it off its flight path? At this point I told Andreas that he had spent so many years as an American citizen, exercising his constitutional rights to freedom of speech, that he failed to see the difference when he spoke as the prime minister of Greece. I was sure that the article in the *Nation* would be retracted (as it was) and, in any event, it was foolish to rely on unsubstantiated speculation to express an official Greek position. Our meeting ended without any retreat on Papandreou's part, but from then on he became less provocative, if not conciliatory, when asked about the Soviets' unwarranted aggression.

Still, Andreas had further damaged his reputation in the Reagan administration, which decided to make known its disapproval at an upcoming NATO meeting in Brussels, in the form of a dressing down by our secretary of state, George Schultz. I was present at their meeting, which was something of an anticlimax. Papandreou was at his most disarming with Schultz, and the two former Californians spent much of the meeting discussing the football rivalry between the University of California and Stanford, where Schultz had taught. When the subject of the Korean passenger jet did arise, Papandreou brushed it off as a misunderstanding of his earlier statements, which were merely an attempt to understand Soviet motives rather than to justify them. As with his predecessor, Alexander Haig, Secretary Schultz found Papandreou a most reasonable fellow—and quite versed on the Stanford-Cal rivalry in the bargain.

Generally speaking, when PASOK's leadership wanted to take the Reagan administration down a peg, it avoided offending the latter's top echelons in Washington. Instead, it made life difficult for the ranks below cabinet level by canceling their appointments and pillorying them in the press when they came to do business in Athens. Such was the case with Assistant Secretary of State for European Affairs Richard Burt when he was about to pay his initial visit to Greece—incautiously scheduled after first visiting Ankara and making a joint statement with the Turkish foreign minister. By all standards it was bland enough but was immediately interpreted as pro-Turkish by the Greeks. On the day of his arrival I was awakened at dawn by a telephone call from Yanni Kapsis, now deputy foreign minister, who informed me that Burt's appointment with the prime minister had been canceled. I protested vigorously that if the government had taken exception to Burt's statements in Ankara, there was all the more reason for Burt to hear the reasons why from Papandreou himself. I then tried repeatedly to reach Andreas by phone but to no avail. Already airborne, Richard Burt diverted his flight to his next destination, Cyprus. The Greek press crowed at PASOK's public rebuff, and the State Department's Bureau of European Affairs seethed at yet another unwarranted affront.

The working level of the Defense Department received similar treatment. While separate visits by Defense Secretary Casper Weinberger and Deputy Secretary Frank Carlucci were amiable enough, no substantive issues were raised, except for Carlucci's suggestion to the prime minister that he might benefit from a briefing on the Pentagon's latest "threat level" of the Soviets' intermediate-range ballistic missiles pointed at Europe. Somewhat to my surprise, Papandreou took him up on the offer, and we shortly arranged for Assistant Secretary of Defense for International Security Affairs Richard Perle to present a detailed assessment of Soviet strength and intentions. Perle's reputation in Greece as an unrepentant Cold Warrior had already made him the subject of several unflattering profiles in the media, and on the day of his arrival Papandreou began to have second thoughts about receiving him. Just as Perle (and two sidekicks bearing slides and diagrams of Soviet missile deployments) were going over their script, I received a call from the prime minister's office that the invitation to Kastri, which included dinner after the briefing, was off. Once again, I immediately called Andreas to protest, and after some arm-twisting, he agreed to hold the briefing but with the proviso that Perle should come alone and limit his briefing to a half hour. The invitation to dinner was not renewed.

Perle knew enough not to go tit for tat over the snub, and he dutifully proceeded to Kastri on his own. He returned shaking his head. Papandreou had shown little interest and asked no questions. Whatever state-of-the-art information he learned from the briefing, it had no effect on his public position. In a subsequent address to PASOK's annual congress he reiterated his theme that, as a socialist, he could only regard the Soviet Union as a peace-loving nation—and the United States as a power bent on pursuing imperialist interests.

Perle's fruitless call on Andreas took place on a Sunday, our household staff's day off, and since I had expected him to dine with Papandreou, I was unprepared when he returned to the residence in a famished state. Alas, my acquaintance with the kitchen was minimal, and Toni had taken Mrs. Perle out to a taverna for the evening. As I groped in the refrigerator for some sort of nourishment, Perle, a gourmet cook as well as a conservative hawk, came to the rescue. In his suitcase was a white truffle (trifola d'Alba) presented to him on his Italian stopover by the president of Piedmont. "There must be some pasta around," he said cheerfully, donning an apron, and in due course we sat down to the best (and certainly most expensive) improvised dinner I have ever had. As we polished off the priceless truffle, we wondered whether Papandreou might have been more receptive to the threat briefing if we'd invited him to join us.

For all this rude behavior, in our respective roles Andreas always separated the political from the personal, and he still liked to chew the fat with me over assorted bureaucratic headaches as if we were still neighbors on Guizi Street. On one occasion he asked for my opinion on the quality of the Greek Foreign Office, which I found as competent as most around the world, but he was not reassured. He was uneasy about his foreign ministry, believing—like most Americans—that one could never trust "elitist" career diplomats. They were inherently conservative, he said, unlike "the people." The minister to the prime minister, a PASOK loyalist to a fault, once commented to me that in the entire Foreign Office there were only two diplomats who were sympathetic to PASOK's objectives. When I asked how he knew this for a fact, he replied, "Because I have read their files." To him, and to Papandreou, I tried to explain that diplomats of all nationalities serve their administrations one at a time, and that it helped them to have a clear understanding of their governments' policies in order to implement them. Speaking as Monty to Andreas, I urged the prime minister to visit the Foreign Ministry, acquaint himself with its organization, and hold briefings with its personnel. He listened politely but never followed up on the suggestion.

This suspicious attitude toward career public servants would continue in other ministries, which PASOK stacked with loyalists at the expense of expertise. Among the elites who would lose the party's support were the technical professionals Andreas had brought from the United States to Greece. By his second term, many had left public service, frustrated by Andreas's unwillingness (or inability) to follow through on government reforms. But by then he was too caught up in an us-versus-them kind of thinking—"them" meaning those elitists who had dominated all Greek institutions and were unrepresentative of The People. Of course The People are as motivated by self-interest as the politicians who court their votes. No government in power wants to alienate its constituents, but the degree to which PASOK curried favor with them was no different from its conservative predecessors.

There were a few occasions when, for political expediency, I, too, needed to court favor with constituent groups at home. These were the Greek Americans, among them the Greek lobby on Capitol Hill, the American-Hellenic Educational and Progressive Association (AHEPA), and the influential Archbishop Iakovos, leader of the Greek Orthodox Church of North and South America. While not part of my diplomatic bailiwick, Greek Americans were loyal to their ancestral homeland, and however disparate their political inclinations they tended to vote en bloc for American politicians who came to Greece's aid in moments of crisis. This was particularly the case in the 1970s, when Congressman John Brademas of Indiana and Senators Paul Sarbanes of Maryland and Paul Tsongas of Massachusetts spearheaded hearings on the Junta dictatorship and its misdeeds. (I should add that the more business-oriented AHEPA, many of whose members had secured lucrative contracts in Greece, avoided passing judgment on the regime.) As for the wily Iakovos, the archbishop always kept his lines open to the powers in Washington, whether Democratic or Republican.

In the 1980s many Greek Americans didn't know what to make of Andreas Papandreou. Liberals applauded his calls for social and financial reforms but found his anti-American rhetoric hypocritical for a man who owed so much to his adopted country. Conservatives disapproved of his unbridled populism and hostility to the Greek Orthodox church. They had not forgotten Andreas's stormy years in exile, when he called Archbishop Iakovos "the spiritual advisor to the Junta" and spurned collaboration with more moderate resistance groups, claiming that they were reactionaries, unworthy of any effort on his part to join forces.

Yet it would have worked to Papandreou's advantage to pay more attention, or at least lip service, to Greek Americans, especially AHEPA, which all previous Greek governments had recognized as a valuable economic asset. It promoted tourism, exports, study in Greece, and cultural exchanges. Furthermore, AHEPA held an annual conference in Athens, where thousands of its members filled hotels and restaurants, shopped extravagantly, and bestowed checks on orphanages and civic organizations. The conference traditionally ended with a gala dinner, at which the prime minister and the American ambassador sat at the head table and toasted to our two countries' historic friendship.

But at AHEPA's annual convention in 1982, Papandreou did not even bother to reply to its invitation. AHEPA's president asked anxiously if I could glean his intentions, which I did by calling Andreas to say that I would be attending the banquet and (hint, hint) looked forward to seeing him there. Still, there was no response, and when I arrived at the banquet the hotel wait staff was removing his chair and place setting from the head table, while the flustered AHEPA president shuffled name cards and the order of speakers. Then, no sooner had we taken our seats than Papandreou's office called the hotel to say that the prime minister would not be attending the dinner but was sending his wife instead. An hour passed. After more shuffling of chairs, and desperate whispers from the kitchen, Margaret made an unhurried entrance and then sat between the notables, making small talk and glancing at her watch, as if waiting for the next bus. This was not like her, but we all have our bad days and at the end of this one she must have been annoyed by the summons to replace her husband at the last moment. Meanwhile, aware that AHEPA had looked askance at my long association with the Papandreous, I gave the most patriotic American speech of my life.

Toni and I had our no-shows as well, the largest being the New York Philharmonic Orchestra, scheduled to perform in the ancient outdoor theater, Herodou Attikou, during the Athens Summer Festival. Tickets were sold out and a clutch of extra kitchen help at the residence were preparing a post-performance buffet for three hundred when a TWA passenger plane at the Athens airport was hijacked by the PLO. Watching news coverage of the hijacking, after their previous performance in Italy, the orchestra members voted unanimously to cancel their Athens visit, leaving our cultural affairs officer (and our kitchen staff) to undo the myriad preparations such large scale visits entail.

The airport's notoriously lax security was a constant concern and led the State Department to issue advisory travel bans on several occasions, with deleterious effects on tourism and Greece's reputation among Western security organizations. Getting the PASOK administration, from Papandreou on down, to address the terrorist threat was an almost impossible task. Its mindset was still in "struggle" mode, willing to downplay or ignore terrorist groups whether homegrown or foreign, on the pretext that they were "freedom fighters" against the establishment in general and the Americans in particular. Our own police work succeeded in identifying several terrorist groups planning attacks in Greece—and in convincing Greek security forces to apprehend them—only to have them "escape" from prison, presumably as the authorities looked the other way. In time, thanks in large measure to my successors' continued pressure (and the number of Greek citizens assassinated) later governments, both PASOK and ND, cracked down on the terrorist scourge. Today the situation has improved but not enough to gain the world's confidence. When Athens hosted the Olympic Games in 2004, most of the security arrangements, and the millions of dollars spent on them, came from the Americans.

Terrorism issues aside, the Reagan administration showed unusual forbearance toward PASOK during its first four years. In foreign relations its bark was proving stronger than its bite. Its economic redistribution policies were spreading wealth among the less privileged, and its social ones were loosening the archaic, stultifying restraints on civil rights that even the most conservative governments in the European Union had long taken for granted. It seemed that Greece was not descending into chaos after all.

A principal reason for Washington's confidence was the fact that Constantine Karamanlis was president of the Hellenic Republic and endorsed by PASOK, and there was every expectation of Parliament reelecting him to a second five-year term in early 1985. I was scheduled to return to Washington for consultations at the time, and before leaving I discussed the upcoming parliamentary vote with

Papandreou, who assured me that Karamanlis had PASOK's total support. I relayed this information to the State Department immediately after arriving in Washington, then checked into my hotel and retired for the night. Early the next morning I received in rapid succession two telephone calls, one from Toni in Athens and the other from the Greek ambassador in Washington. Both brought the startling news that in a stormy parliamentary session an overwhelming number of PASOK deputies had refused to reelect Karamanlis. Toni, who was meeting friends near Syntagma Square, had dashed home to call me on a secure phone and to describe the public uproar outside Parliament as the news spread. Forgoing breakfast I bolted to the State Department to discuss the matter with the Greek Desk officer. As we pondered this turn of events, I received a third telephone call, this time from a total stranger who identified himself as an oil company executive, bearing an urgent message to me from Andreas Papandreou. This was the stuff of a bad movie, but I listened to the caller's explanation that the prime minister wanted to keep his message confidential and had instructed his mysterious conduit to dictate it to me verbatim.

It was an unconvincing message, the gist of which was that Andreas had never intended to mislead me about PASOK's position and had been totally surprised by its rank and file's hostile rejection of Karamanlis. Under such pressure, he concluded his message, surely I would understand that he had no choice but to yield to popular will.

Surely, I thought to the contrary, this was not the whole story, if only because it was unlikely that Andreas could be so unaware of his deputies' intentions. It was more likely that Karamanlis's ouster was some sort of internal political compromise between the hard-left and moderate PASOK factions that would not affect the government's external policies in any dramatic way. But to a succession of American administrations Karamanlis had been a trusted and much respected figure for thirty years, and the mood in Washington was that we should indicate our disapprobation at a high level. With the announcement that the new president would be Christos Sartzetakis, a former judge with impeccable left-wing credentials, the moment seemed right. The Greek government (and much of the press) was well aware that I was in Washington when Karamanlis was jettisoned, and a call on President Reagan would drive home the point that he was paying attention to the drama unfolding in Athens.

He wasn't really, but Ronald Reagan had read about anti-Americanism in Greece and was curious to know the cause. This gave me the chance to explain that, in my opinion, anti-Americanism in Greece was often the flip side of underlying pro-American sentiment—caused not so much by a rejection of American values but by disappointed expectations. Although those expectations could be exaggerated and unrealistic, I thought that most Greeks basically believed in keeping a close relationship with the United States, just not so close as to make them feel that Greece was a perpetual client state. The next day, in more detailed discussion with members of the National Security Council, I reiterated my belief that Papandreou neither intended nor could afford to leave NATO or the EU, but needed to assert that if Greece were to remain in the Western camp, it would do so of its own choosing, in its own way. As with most of Papandreou's provocative statements against the West, they were gestures, not any real commitment to join the nonaligned nations, much less the Soviet bloc. By temperament and education, however, he always tended to believe that a kind of fuzzy, Third World order would prove the solution to the world's problems,

Our gesture to him was a small but visible diplomatic rebuff: I stayed in Washington until after the Greek National Day ceremonies, presided over by Sartzetakis, and my absence in the ambassadorial row of seats was duly noted. After my return I called on both Papandreou and Ambassador Petros Molyviatis, chief of staff and close confidant of former president Karamanlis. Not surprisingly, their accounts of Karamanlis's ouster were diametrically opposed. Andreas lamely reiterated his confidential message to me, adding a personal anecdote that even his barber had declared that a second Karamanlis presidency would be a betrayal of PASOK's ideals. Molyviatis, on the other hand, accused Papandreou of deliberate misrepresentation, not just to me but to Karamanlis himself. Up to the last minute he had the prime minister's word that his reelection was assured, all the while Papandreou knowing that Sartzetakis was secretly waiting in the wings. Making allowance for Molyviatis's fierce loyalty to his boss, I concluded that he may have exaggerated the prime minister's assurances to Karamanlis, but I never understood why Papandreou made the same assurances to me. He could have said nothing. He could have said that the situation was fluid, but the last thing he should have done was to put himself in such an embarrassing position, admitting that he was out of touch with his own party on an issue of central importance to it. It only confirmed outside opinion that he wasn't governing Greece so much as pandering to PASOK's rank and file.

Out of touch with his party or not, and I didn't think he was, I did think that Papandreou's political acumen was becoming dulled by the grind of administrative duties (never his forte) and by outside distractions. By then he and Margaret were leading separate lives ("Two strangers under the same roof," he confessed openly to us), and he had begun a clandestine affair with Dimitra Liani. At the same time, to fulfill his promise to bring prosperity and a welfare state to the masses, he was recklessly overdrawing on the EU cash cow and state coffers to do so, spreading doubts about his economic acumen as well. In his second term these doubts were confirmed by mounting national debt and financial scandals, which would dominate the headlines as much as his marital ones and cost him the 1989 election. But throughout his first term he retained his popularity by tacking this way and that on foreign policy and putting money into the pockets of the average citizen without creating revenue through taxes or trade. So much for his "scientific" approach to building a modern economy based on "the entrepreneurial state," free from political interference, and combining public/private investment with the technical know-how to develop Greece's natural resources.

Papandreou's real strength was in the fact that he looked to the future, not the past, and in creating a more egalitarian polity in

Greece he filled the void that had always been lacking in Greek politics: the establishment of a modern, leftist, noncommunist party on a par with democratic socialist parties that had existed in Western Europe since the nineteenth century. Papandreou's social welfare programs—however profligate—brought Greece closer to European living standards and soon accustomed Greek voters to judge subsequent governments by how well or poorly they maintained them.

In the process, Greeks finally put aside the anachronistic issues that had characterized political debate from independence through the civil war. Karamanlis had taken the first steps by allowing communist parties back into the political system, and Andreas went even further. One of his first executive actions was to grant amnesty to Greek communists who had fled to the Eastern bloc after the civil war, restore their citizenship, and invite them back to the homeland. Conservative objections were based not so much on principle but on the cost of paying them pensions, health care coverage, and the like.

Andreas's principal failures lay in his perpetration of Greece's corrupt political practices. "If you want to lick the system you have to join it," he once told me candidly, which came to mean winning elections in the overwrought style playing the Messiah. In the 1981 campaign, there was a running joke about PASOK candidates' extravagant promises to the rubes. Candidate: "We will bring you schools!! We will bring you roads!! We will bring you bridges!" Rubes, scratching their heads: "But we don't have a river!" Candidate: "We will bring you a river!"

But if not rivers, PASOK did bring schools and roads and hospitals to the rubes, and Papandreou's popularity soared in consequence. Andreas also changed constrictive laws on individual rights. In a move strongly opposed by the church, and spearheaded by Margaret Papandreou, PASOK introduced civil marriage, decriminalized adultery, abolished (in theory) the dowry system, and legalized the sale of contraceptives.

These reforms carried Papandreou to victory in the 1985 elections, although his percentage of the vote dropped slightly from

48 percent to 45 percent, while PASOK's number of parliamentary seats declined from 172 to 161. With 126 seats, New Democracy garnered almost 41 percent of the popular vote, a gain of 11 percent since 1981. KKE-Exterior (Stalinist faction) won under 10 percent of the vote and 12 seats, while KKE-Interior (Euro-Communist faction) limped behind with a single seat. Over a dozen other parties with names ranging from the Patriotic Right to the Trotskyists, the Fighting Socialists, and the Enlightenment Movement won no seats but at least preserved the Greek tradition of spawning multiple, idiosyncratic parties of one.

Then the downward spiral began in earnest. By his second term Papandreou was unashamedly reverting to the politics of patronage and cronyism that he had so despaired of when he first returned to Greece. As budget deficits skyrocketed and challengers within PASOK came to the fore (shades of the Center Union), he retreated into a world of sycophantic courtiers and crooked financiers. Between his now public liaison with Dimitra Liani and an embezzlement scandal known as the "Koskotas Affair," the tabloids had a field day, and his defeat in the next election was virtually guaranteed. In 1988 Andreas was indicted by Parliament for his involvement in a $200 million embezzlement scheme, in which he ordered (or at least endorsed) state utility companies to transfer their holdings to the failing Bank of Crete, owned by his personal friend, George Koskotas. Koskotas, already under indictment for embezzling millions from the bank, claimed that Papandreou himself had received $6 million in exchange for the bailout. Along with his deputy minister and two former ministers, a defiant but by then ailing Andreas was tried in absentia. He was acquitted by a single vote. His cronies went to jail.

Having left Athens in late 1985, after the start of Papandreou's second administration, I followed his decline and fall from afar, as I did the Greek political scene when New Democracy returned to power. Like most outside observers, I was astonished when Andreas, despite the critical state of his health, managed to defeat his archenemy Constantine Mitsotakis in the October 1993 general election.

He clung to office, ineffectually, until advanced heart and lung disease forced him to retire in January 1996, only six months before his death in June of that year.

Three years earlier, in 1993, when Mitsotakis, the Center Union apostate, was New Democracy's prime minister, I visited Andreas on a swing through the Mediterranean in conjunction with a book I was writing after my retirement from the Foreign Service. On an earlier visit in 1990, I had found him extremely frail, confined to bed with a monitor taped to his arm. But this time he seemed somewhat stronger, still thin and ashen but still head of PASOK and—amazingly—preparing to run in the fall elections.

After the visit I made a memorandum of our conversation, excerpts of which I now draw on to record his thoughts in the waning years of his life. Dimitra and he were living in a rented house in the northern suburb of Ekali, while a newly purchased one was being remodeled. He apologized that he could not receive me in the latter (later ridiculed as the "Pink Palace"), saying, "But you know how long women can take about these things." He seemed to accept the role of compliant husband, acquiescing for example to the exigencies of Dimitra's personal grooming. That day she was with a masseuse, then getting her hair done, and would not be joining us. As in 1990 I sensed that Andreas preferred not to introduce his third wife to friends who had known his second, and the photographs displayed in his study were only of her and his grandchildren.

We talked briefly about my travels and the recent death of my mother, whom he remembered from Carmel. This led him to reminisce about his own mother, and how he still regretted that she had not lived long enough to see him become a two-term prime minister. As for a third, Andreas said candidly, "This will be my last chance, and we will need a *national* government, not just a party one." I asked who might be the best talent in both parties to form a cabinet, to which he replied, without naming names, that there were "certain people on both right and left who could make a contribution."

Thinking of PASOK stalwarts like former education minister Gerasimos Arsenis and Costas Simitis, who had served as minister of agriculture and minister of national economy, I asked casually whom Andreas might choose among PASOK's current leaders. He bristled at the question. "Leaders? What leaders? To the country at large they are unknown," he said dismissively. "They are never interviewed by the press and they never appear on television." In fact, Simitis would succeed Papandreou after his death, but it was clear that Andreas wasn't about to pass the torch. The only person qualified to run the government, he confided, was his close collaborator and former minister of the interior, labor, and health during PASOK's eight years of governance, George Yennimatas. "Unfortunately," he added, "Yennimatas is dying of cancer."[2]

He then launched into a somber review of Greece's internal and external problems and how badly his old nemesis, Prime Minister Mitsotakis, was handling them. "Monty, I have never known a man like Mitsotakis. He is completely empty, completely without values. He has no ideology; he simply lives from day to day. As for that Foreign Minister (Michalis) Papaconstantinou, you have known him a long time. You know he is not up to the job."[3]

I disagreed. Papaconstantinou was an old friend. I had just heard him speak at Panteion University and was struck by how ably and calmly he fielded tough questions on the feud between Greece and (Slav) Macedonia over the latter's use of the name.[4] I asked why every Greek political party was trying to outdo the others in driving Macedonia into the arms of rival nations. It was a tiny new country, dependent in many ways on Athens. How did it serve Greek interests to lessen that relationship and increase its dependence on others? Andreas said only that Mitsotakis had played his cards badly and failed to present the Greek case convincingly to the world. This led to a brief *tour d'horizon* of the Balkans and their current troubles, but Andreas's principal preoccupation was with the European Union and how badly he had been treated by it. "I am completely disillusioned with the Western Europeans," he said, "especially with their hostility to Greece. Their anti-Greek attitude is rampant. No one supplies leadership. No one looks ahead." By this time, of course, Andreas's reputation in the EU was at a nadir, both as an economist and a politician.

The remainder of our conversation touched on the Clinton administration and, ironically, growing American isolationism. "Well," I said, paraphrasing Richard Nixon's comment to the press when he lost a governor's race in California, "at least you won't have America to kick around anymore." Before I left, we returned to family matters, and I told Andreas that his eldest son George, who had recently been a fellow at Harvard's Center for International Affairs, had represented Greece well, and that his father could be proud of him. Sadly, like his own father before him, Andreas had a troubled relationship with his eldest son, and my compliment elicited a grimace. "At least *that*," he said, without further comment.[5]

He looked tired. Over two hours had passed, and I rose to go. Despite his shuffled gait, Andreas insisted on accompanying me to the door and then down the walk to my car. As I started to shake his hand he leaned forward, as if asking me to embrace him. Then he walked slowly back to the front door, turned, and waved goodbye for the last time.

Epilogue

LARGER-THAN-LIFE political figures are both instantly recognizable and ultimately unknowable. Their admirers turn them into holy icons and their detractors into derogatory cartoons. Because the Greeks always called Papandreou by his first name, his critics often compared him to Fidel Castro. But while chants of "Andreas" in Athens became as familiar as chants of "Fidel" in Havana, the two men were more dissimilar than alike. Castro was a genuine revolutionary and a committed communist. Andreas began, and ended, as a socialist, but he was never a communist, much as he claimed (in Trotskyite fashion) that because the Soviet Union was not a capitalist society it could never be an imperial one like the United States.

He was not thinking of nineteenth-century European imperialism but of United States dominance in the twentieth, after World War II, when political and geographical divisions pitted communism against capitalism in the ideological battles of the Cold War. The Soviets created virtual colonies in Eastern Europe and Castro's Cuba; the Americans created alliances, both military and economic, and in the case of threatened, impoverished Greece, the United States played an outsized role in propping up its shaky democratic institutions.

Had those institutions been sturdier, there would have been no proclivity to turn Greece into what Andreas vehemently decried as a "client state," and it is true that even as the United States drastically reduced its economic aid, it continued to wield considerable influence over Greece's political system. Andreas burst onto the Greek political stage like an arsonist setting fire in a crowded theater, but had the theater not been so flimsy it would have taken more than his inflammatory rhetoric to ignite it. Much of the blame must be shared by political leaders in the decades before, both conservative and liberal, who failed to bring real reforms to the political system. For all Papandreou's social reforms, he used the same system to enact them. To some extent he was simply adapting to the circumstances he inherited, but his pledge to revolutionize Greek politics produced no revolutionary results, however much the transition to a socialist state remained his intellectual ideal.

No country has ever achieved true socialism, which in Marxist thinking eliminates the class system and ultimately the political establishment. Andreas, too, always harbored ideas of an egalitarian society, but they were as abstract as his economic formulations— theoretical models that even he never tried to put into practice. By the time he was prime minister, whatever notions he entertained of the state as an economic power, supplanting the private sector, they proved as unrealistic as Marx's claim that "scientific" socialism would "plot the curve of history."

For Andreas, the curve of history was more like a roller coaster, a series of dizzying ups and downs. First a Trotskyite, then an American liberal democrat and author of a "scientific" and "apolitical" study on the Greek economy, he eased into centrist Greek politics as his father's advisor, then into hard-knuckle politics as George Papandreou's fierce opponent. Challenging his father's too timid approach to his radical reform policies, Andreas ran successfully for office on a platform to overthrow the old establishment. The irony (and dismay) was not lost on George Papandreou. In a 1990 interview I conducted with the Cypriot politician Vassos Lyssarides, he recalled the elder Papandreou's bitterness toward his son. "Why does he call for the overthrow of the establishment? Doesn't he realize that I *am* the establishment?"

The word carried more political freight in Greece than in the United States, where a more mobile and prosperous society could attack the establishment without inciting anarchy or the downfall of American democracy. In the years Andreas lived in the United States, critics freely discussed how to decrease the establishment's influence, or even take it over themselves, because Americans of all stripes regularly moved in and out of it, and change—whether political, economic, or social—was a matter of degree, not destruction of the social fabric. This was not the case in Greece, where, historically, both liberal and conservative politicians united to preserve the status quo. Occasionally they were toppled by right-wing dictators but never by socialists or communists lurking in their midst. The Greek establishment saw the left as an existential threat; by comparison, Andreas's critiques of the American status quo were closer to the normal political activities that he and Margaret had engaged in at Minnesota and Berkeley.

But Greece was also in transition. A majority of politically underrepresented Greeks came to support Andreas's anti-establishment views, particularly the working class and the younger generation. His popularity would surpass his father's in the rural areas, where the patronage system was rife, with local politicians handing out favors (letters of recommendation, debt cancellations, and the like) in exchange for the constituents' votes.

As they had done under the Ottomans, Greeks of all stations entrusted their well-being to family cohesion, including entrenched political families, a tradition that favored the group over the individual. But Greek individualism, as I once wrote in a dispatch to the State Department, grows like crabgrass between the flagstones of Greek conformity. It ranges from raising chickens on an apartment balcony to the enduring presence of green grocers and specialty shops in the age of supermarkets and chain stores. But rarely had these individual, entrepreneurial efforts been harnessed to national ones, as they have been in less culturally cloistered societies like the United States.

The American side of Andreas recognized the strengths of individualism. As he wrote in 1954, American society "was built on belief in the individual as the basis for its success." When he was still an economist, Andreas and I discussed the possible ways in which that crabgrass could be transformed into green lawns in his native land. But over the course of his conversion back to Greekness (and socialism) Andreas had come to view the success of American individualism (and capitalism) in a negative light, as components of American imperialism. From then on he eschewed Greek individualism and pitched his campaigns for reform to "the people," an indistinguishable mass he would rally to restore Greece's proper place in the world. Looking back on his campaign platforms, "Out of PASOK! Out of the EU! Greece for the Greeks!" I see them today as his call for a *national* individualism, free from subservience to the United States and indeed all members of the Western alliance. In that sense, Papandreou was as nationalist as the two dictatorships that had imprisoned him in 1939 and 1967.

This patriotic rhetoric, I believe, was also based on Andreas's need to establish his Greek credentials, certainly during his 1974 campaign when many voters regarded him as an interloper. Many called him an imposter; what had he ever done for Greece except stir up trouble? And what Greek would ever betray his own father? Other critics bruited it about that he was actually working for the CIA, pretending to disown his adopted country for nefarious purposes yet to be revealed. A psychiatrist friend probably came closest to the real Andreas by calling him a man filled with inner conflicts.

Few people go through life without periods of inner conflicts, but Andreas's life, from childhood on, was one of suppressing them. This behavior gave him a kind of nervous energy (I remember him pacing more than sitting down) but also mood swings and inconsistent actions, none more than when he had to choose between his Greek and American identities. During his first term as prime minister, Andreas's handling of Greek-American relations brought out his American pragmatism. In any case, he had to focus on his vast domestic agenda of social reform, unfortunately at the cost of political and financial ones. Whether he ever intended to tackle them became moot during his second term of office, by which time his party was split, the bills overdue, and to stay in power the once reformist zealot fell back on the same cronyism and financial chicanery of the old political establishment he had vowed to abolish.

In assessing Andreas Papandreou's place in modern Greek history, I begin with the premise that he was both highly intelligent and inherently rational. But he was also shallow in his convictions and a vacillator, lacking the steely spine needed to bring lasting governmental and financial reforms to Greece. In the end, PASOK turned out to be just another political party, as eclipsed today as Papandreou's own reputation.

Nevertheless, the Greece that Papandreou left behind was significantly different from the one that came before. This older Greece was closer to a feudal society than a modern democracy, despite Constantine Karamanlis's efforts to drag it into the twentieth century and the European Economic Community. His conservative constituents were less forward-thinking than he but would never dream of voting for any leftward-leaning parties, which they considered as dangerous as the communists. With politics so polarized, the noncommunist left and the communists were strange bedfellows, but it was the only bed available to them.

In this respect, PASOK's most important contribution was to separate the two once and for all, providing left-wing parties a proper place in the political spectrum. The effect was to shorten Greece's long and painful convalescence from the trauma of the 1945–49 civil war and to put an end to the anachronistic divisions that had long dominated the configuration of the main political parties.

In comparison to my early years in Athens, Greek politics, while still as noisy as the Greeks themselves, have progressed to debating contemporary issues of globalization, immigration, and the fiscal austerity program imposed on Greece by the EU to repay debts incurred by the 2008 financial crisis. While all parties greedily ran up the debt, it was begun under Papandreou's lavish welfare programs that encouraged the Greeks to believe they were richer than they actually were. Neither Andreas Papandreou, the respected economist, nor his successors were about to disillusion them, and so structural political and financial reforms, especially tax reforms, were left for another day.

Andreas could, and should, have done more in all these areas. Why didn't he? Perhaps this gifted Greek suppressed his unworkable economic theories as deeply as his Trotskyite beliefs when he entered Harvard. Perhaps ill health and the deterioration of his marriage contributed to his inaction; or perhaps, like his father, he was simply better at opposing than governing. Even in his first term I detected signs of ennui, a certain lack of interest in following through on the job. For years he had expended prodigious energy to prove himself to his father, to his academic peers, and to the Greek electorate. Perhaps he felt there was nothing left to prove.

His failures have been recorded by legions of critics, myself included. But someone had to broaden the narrow political choices that had been foisted on Greek voters since the country's independence. Andreas was the first to do so, and despite his reckless expenditures, he established social welfare programs that had been standard in Western Europe for over a century. Today even the most conservative Greek politicians wouldn't dismantle them, and the main debates with their opponents are about who can administer the system more efficiently.

Like most politicians who reach the pinnacle, Andreas Papandreou was Janus-faced, both an idealist and an opportunist. In his youth he inveighed against Greece's corrupt political establishment only to adopt its methods in his desire to create a more egalitarian society. Probably no one person could have achieved a total overhaul of the Greek political system, but he could have upheld the goal by starting the process. Instead, he rose—and clung—to power through unbridled populism and the cult of personality still evident in Greek politics today. This mixed reputation as both a reformer and a renegade may well be the sum of Andreas Papandreou's legacy to Greece.

Notes

1. The Past Is Never the Past

1. Margaret Papandreou, *Nightmare in Athens* (Englewood Cliffs NJ: Prentice Hall, 1970), 103–4.

2. Christina Rassia, *Theka Chronia Syzigos tou Andrea Papandreou* [Ten Years the Wife of Andreas Papandreou] (Athens: Xenophon Press, 1992), 62.

3. Sir John Maynard, *Russia in Flux* (New York: MacMillan Company, 1948), 111.

4. *Pondiki* is a satirical weekly published in Athens, the Greek equivalent of the British *Private Eye* or the French *Le Canard Enchainé*. Like the latter periodicals it has a reputation for accurate investigative journalism as well as savage satire. Immediately after the death of Andreas Papandreou, *Pondiki* published a supplement on his life, most of the material being drawn from its own files.

5. "Andreas, 1919–1958: Apo tin Athena stin Ameriki" [Andreas, 1919–1958: From Athens to America], *Pondiki* newspaper supplement, June 26, 1996, 15.

6. Alba Ambert, ed., *Every Greek Has a Story* (Athens, Greece: Athens College Press, 1992), 25–26.

7. Michael Macrakis, *To Xekinima* (Athens, Greece: Katoptro Publishers, 2000), 18.

8. Homer W. Davis, *The Story of Athens College: The First Thirty-Five Years* (Athens, Greece: Athens College Press, 1992), 8.

9. Davis, *Story of Athens College*, 148.

10. Davis, *Story of Athens College*, 149–50.

11. Macrakis, *To Xekinima*, 26. The author quotes from an interview with Papandreou conducted by the journalist Petros Efthymiou published in the periodical *Tachydromos*, August 1994.

12. Plebiscites on the Greek royal family traditionally registered results conforming to the preference of the government in power. Perhaps the most fairly conducted and therefore the most accurate was the plebiscite of December 1974, held by the Karamanlis government after the fall of the military junta the previous summer. Roughly one-third of those who voted in the plebiscite favored the return of the king and two-thirds opposed it.

13. *Pondiki*, June 25, 1996, 15.

14. Macrakis, *To Xekinima*, 36–37.

15. Macrakis, *To Xekinima*, 37–38.

16. André Gide, *Retour de l'URSS* (Paris: Gallimard, 1936).

17. *Pondiki*, June 26, 1996, 16. The appeal of Trotskyism to Marxists in a country like Greece was not only that it seemed more "democratic" than Stalinism but that it suggested the feasibility of revolution in preindustrial societies.

18. C. M. Woodhouse, *The Story of Modern Greece* (London: Faber and Faber, 1968); Richard Clogg, *A Short History of Modern Greece* (New York: Cambridge University Press, 1979).

19. Andreas Papandreou, *Democracy at Gunpoint: The Greek Front* (Garden City NY: Doubleday & Company, 1970), 43–44.

20. He later told his first wife, Christina, that the apartment was useful for personal reasons as well. This may have been a boast.

21. A. Papandreou, *Democracy at Gunpoint*, 44–45.

22. The day celebrating the birth of the saint after whom one is named, an occasion more often commemorated in Greece than a birthday.

23. Rassia, *Theka Chronia*, 67.

24. Macrakis, *To Xekinima*, 64.

25. A. Papandreou, *Democracy at Gunpoint*, 44.

26. *Pondiki*, June 26, 1996, 16.

27. *Pondiki*, June 26, 1996, 16.

28. Lagoudakis later joined the State Department and was for many years the senior Greek specialist in the department's Office of Intelligence and Research (INR).

2. Building a Future

1. *Pondiki*, June 26, 1996, 16–17

2. Rassia, *Theka Chronia Syzigos tou Andrea Papandreou*. This interesting and often-revealing account of Rassia's life with Papandreou during his first ten years in the United States has never been published in English, although this was the language in which she wrote it. A Greek edition was apparently printed in the years of Papandreou's premiership, but all copies were kept out of circulation, reportedly because at Papandreou's direction they were bought up and destroyed. Only after Papandreou's death in 1996 did a hastily translated and pirated edition appear in Athens. The retranslation into English is by the present author.

3. Rassia, *Theka Chronia*, 50–51.

4. Conversation with Paul Mitarachis, May 16, 1998.

5. Rassia, *Theka Chronia*, 50–57.

6. Rassia, *Theka Chronia*, 55.

7. Rassia, *Theka Chronia*, 59.

8. Rassia, *Theka Chronia*, 71.

9. Rassia, *Theka Chronia*, 78.

10. Rassia, *Theka Chronia*, 69.

11. Rassia, *Theka Chronia*, 71.

12. Rassia, *Theka Chronia*, 72.

13. Rassia, *Theka Chronia*, 76.

14. Rassia, *Theka Chronia*, 81.

15. Rassia, *Theka Chronia*, 100.

16. Rassia, *Theka Chronia*, 101.

17. It is somewhat misleading to speak of a Greek upper class, although in periods of monarchical rule the circles around the palace assumed something of an aristocratic status. A few families were awarded titles by the Italians when they ruled the Ionian Islands but only die-hard monarchists took them seriously. As a political group royalists were as diverse as the Venizelists, ranging all the way from peasants to oligarchs. That said, Greece is essentially a nonhierarchical society in the sense that deference to rank and wealth go against the Greek democratic instincts. I once played a round of golf with a former Greek prime minister who at one hole flubbed his approach shot. He turned irritably to his caddy and said, "Don't move when I take my back swing." The caddy took a drag on his cigarette and replied, "I didn't move. You made a lousy shot."

18. Macrakis, *To Xekinima*, 76–77.

19. *Pondiki*, June 26, 1996, 17.

20. Adolph A. Berle and Gardiner C. Means, *The Modern Corporation and Private Property* (New York: MacMillan & Company, 1932 and 1939).

21. Andreas G. Papandreou, "The Location and Scope of the Entrepreneurial Function" (PhD diss., Harvard University Archives, Call Number GU90.4435A, 1943), 36.

22. A. Papandreou, "Location and Scope," 33–34.

23. A. Papandreou, "Location and Scope," 36.

24. A. Papandreou, "Location and Scope," 34–35.

25. A. Papandreou, "Location and Scope," summary of thesis, 7.

26. Rassia, *Theka Chronia*, 99–100.

27. Rassia, *Theka Chronia*, 110.

28. Rassia, *Theka Chronia*, 110.

29. Papandreou's periods of training and subsequent assignments as a pharmacist's mate cannot be reconstructed with precision. According to the office of Military Personnel Records of the National Personnel Records Center in St. Louis, Missouri, the repository for files of all retired American military personnel, Papandreou's service records, along with many others', were incinerated by a fire that destroyed a portion of the archives on July 12, 1973. (Letter to author, dated March 15, 2004, from Archives Technician George Buford of the National Personnel Records Center).

30. *Pondiki*, June 26, 1996, 7.

31. Interview with Nick Papandreou, October 7, 1996.

32. Rassia, *Theka Chronia*, 128.

3. Personal and Postwar Developments

1. Rassia, *Theka Chronia*, 125–27.

2. Interview with Nick Papandreou, October 7, 1996.

3. It is not unusual for Greek Americans, even those whose parents are native-born citizens of the United States, to find themselves fighting off draft notices from the Greek military if they return to Greece for a visit.

4. Rassia, *Theka Chronia*, 136.

5. Macrakis, *To Xekinima*, 143–44.

6. Whatever chagrin Andreas may have felt about his situation at Harvard, his personal relations with Alexander were cordial. Alexander states that he and his wife earned the Papandreous' gratitude by turning over to them a small apartment at 52 Dunster Street in Cambridge when the Alexanders moved to larger quarters as they awaited the arrival of a new baby. (Telephone conversation with Sidney Alexander, May 28, 1998.)

7. Rassia, *Theka Chronia*, 139.

8. Macrakis, *To Xekinima*, 141.

9. In her own memoir, Margaret Papandreou says he was offered an "associate" professorship, but this seems too high a jump for an instructor with only one year's experience on the job and no significant published work to his credit. It is more likely that when Andreas moved to the University of Minnesota, he was put on the tenure track to become an associate professor.

10. Rassia, *Theka Chronia*, 140.

11. Rassia, *Theka Chronia*, 140.

4. Romance and Return

1. M. Papandreou, *Nightmare in Athens*, 14.

2. Andreas's half brother was a decade younger than Andreas. Margaret was told that young George had been afflicted by encephalitis as an infant. He had a troubled life of unfinished schools, unsuccessful jobs, and failed suicide attempts. Although never cut off from the Papandreou family, he became increasingly estranged from Andreas—at whose funeral service in 1996 George struck a strangely discordant note amidst the eulogies by lamenting that his brother had never loved him.

3. Rassia, *Theka Chronia*, 142.

4. In a television interview in 1983 Margaret was asked by Diane Sawyer whether in her youth she had ever dreamed that one day she would be the wife of the Greek prime minister. "No," replied Margaret, "I dreamed of being prime minister myself."

5. Rassia, *Theka Chronia*, 144.

6. M. Papandreou, *Nightmare in Athens*, 18–19.

7. Rassia, *Theka Chronia*, 144–46.

8. See Andreas G. Papandreou, "Market Structure and Monopoly Power," *American Economic Review* (September 1949): 883–97.

9. Interview with Nick Papandreou, October 26, 1996.

10. A. G. Papandreou, "Economics and the Social Sciences," *Economic Journal* 60, no. 240 (December 1950): 720.

11. A. G. Papandreou, "Economics and the Social Sciences," 723.

12. Rassia, *Theka Chronia*, 157–59.

13. Rassia, *Theka Chronia*, 159–60.

14. Adamantios Pepelasis, *Stin Akri tou Aiona* [At the End of the Century] (Athens: Castaniotis, 1996), 122. Pepelasis met Andreas Papandreou in Berkeley in 1955. They became close friends and collaborated in the creation of the Economic Research Center in Athens. That was an intermediate step that led eventually to Papandreou's permanent return to Greece in 1963.

15. Pepelasis, *Stin Akri tou Aiona*, 206.

16. Rassia, *Theka Chronia*, 156.

17. Rassia, *Theka Chronia*, 167.

18. Pepelasis, *Stin Akri tou Aiona*, 206.

19. Andreas G. Papandreou and J. T. Wheeler, *Competition and Its Regulation* (New York: Prentice-Hall, Inc., 1954).

20. Papandreou and Wheeler, *Competition and Its Regulation*, 284–89.

21. Papandreou and Wheeler, *Competition and Its Regulation*, 11.

22. Pepelasis, *Stin Akri tou Aiona*, 202.

23. Henry Rosovsky, Geyser University Professor, Emeritus, and former provost of Harvard. Interview, May 16, 1998.

24. The most recent being Daniel McFadden in 2000; Professor Dale Jorgensen, telephone conversation, January 21, 2006.

25. Rosovsky interview, May 16, 1998.

26. Margaret Papandreou, interview, February 21, 1998.

27. Margaret Papandreou, interview, May 29, 1997.

5. The Years of Our Greek Experience

1. Nicholas Papandreou, *A Crowded Heart* (New York: Picador, 1996), 3.

2. Margaret Papandreou interview, May 29, 1997.

3. Margaret Papandreou interview, May 29, 1997.

4. Christina Rassia, *Theka Chronia*, 60.

5. A. Papandreou, *Democracy at Gunpoint*, 105–8; M. Papandreou, *Nightmare in Athens*, 56–60.

6. M. Papandreou, *Nightmare in Athens*, 67.

7. Dispatch No. 619, classified "confidential," *A Winter of Our Discontent: Some Implications of the Current Political Maneuvering in Greece*, dated March 13, 1962. Department of Central Files 781 00/3 2662 (*Foreign Relations of the United States*, Vol. 16).

8. Carl Kaysen interview, July 15, 1999.

9. M. Papandreou, *Nightmare in Athens*, 61.

8. Prime Time

1. For additional details on Papandreou's flirtation with nonalignment, see Richard L. Jackson, *The Non-Aligned, the UN, and the Superpowers* (New York: Praeger Publishers, 1983), 83, 144, and 230.

2. George Yennimatas, PASOK Minister of the Interior, 1981–84.

3. Michalis Papaconstantinou, Minister of Foreign Affairs, 1992–93.

4. Greek governments have refused to recognize the former Yugoslav Republic of Macedonia as "Macedonia," fearing it will lead to expansionist claims on the northern Greek region of the same name.

5. George Papandreou would later serve admirably as foreign minister, then prime minister himself until the catastrophic Greek financial crisis (begun by Andreas) brought him down.

Related ADST Book Series Titles

Raising the Flag: Adventures of America's First Envoys in Faraway Lands
Peter D. Eicher

Behind Embassy Walls: The Life and Times of an American Diplomat
Brandon Grove

Captive in the Congo: A Consul's Return to the Heart of Darkness
Michael P. E. Hoyt
Introduction by Monteagle Stearns

The Incidental Oriental Secretary and Other Tales of Foreign Service
Richard L. Jackson

*The Colonels' Coup and the American Embassy: A Diplomat's View of the
Breakdown of Democracy in Cold War Greece*
Robert V. Keeley

American Ambassadors: The Past, Present, and Future of America's Diplomats
Dennis C. Jett

American Diplomats: The Foreign Service at Work
William Morgan and C. Stuart Kennedy

Witness to a Changing World
David D. Newsom

The Craft of Political Analysis for Diplomats
Raymond F. Smith

For a complete list of series titles, visit adst.org/publication.